The Ninth Grade Opportunity: Transforming Schools from the Bottom Up

Scott Habeeb, Ray Moore and Alan Seibert

iUniverse, Inc.
New York   Bloomington

The Ninth Grade Opportunity:
Transforming Schools from the Bottom Up

iUniverse books may be ordered through booksellers or by contacting:

iUniverse
1663 Liberty Drive
Bloomington, IN 47403
www.iuniverse.com
1-800-Authors (1-800-288-4677)

ISBN: 978-0-595-48472-0 (pbk)
ISBN: 978-0-595-71990-7 (cloth)
ISBN: 978-0-595-60564-4 (ebk)

Printed in the United States of America

iUniverse rev. date: 12/15/2008

Foreword

With over a decade of experience in transitioning thousands of ninth grade students from "just first year high school students" to students whose odds have been increased for completing high school, Habeeb, Moore and Seibert describe not only how they succeeded but also how others might learn from their insights. The authors also make a convincing case that their teaming approach to helping ninth graders become better students also helped them become better teachers – teachers who built both personal and professional support systems for themselves during the process. Through their teaming, these teachers learned to mentor their students and each other. As a result, they did not experience the "burn out" that many ninth grade teachers experience.

Although they describe primarily what they did and how they did it, because the authors have worked with hundreds of teachers in other schools, they recognize that "standardizing expectations for ninth grade students" is important; they also contend that differences and adaptations have to be made, based on varying school schedules, student needs, and local policies. A paraphrased sentence that we remember well is that there is no universal solution to the Grade 9 challenge, but there is a nearly universal process for making the needed changes. It is the process described in this book that the reader will appreciate.

This book is easy to read. We particularly like the Personal Voices that appear throughout the text. Those voices give both meaning and depth to the authors' message. We highly recommend careful study of Chapter 11. It is a "nuts and bolts" chapter that educators will find helpful in revamping programs for students in Grade 9 – the "Make It or Break It Year" for thousands of students throughout the United States.

Prepared by: Robert Lynn Canady, Professor Emeritus, University of Virginia, and Nancy R. Iverson, Assistant Dean, School of Professional Studies, University of Virginia.

Acknowledgments

The authors would like to acknowledge the City of Salem Schools in Salem, Virginia, for the role that the school system has played in the authors' professional lives. The City of Salem Schools has provided the authors with a supportive environment in which to practice the greatest of all professions, teaching and impacting young people. The authors would like to thank the City of Salem School Board and Central Administration for overseeing such a dynamic school system. The authors would also like to acknowledge Mr. John Hall, Mrs. Betsy McClearn, and the other administrators that have led Salem High School over the years. Their vision, their pursuit of excellence, and their willingness to take chances on the ideas of others, have empowered the authors to in turn take chances as they look for new ways to better meet the needs of students.

Contents

Foreword..v

Acknowledgments vii

Preface...xi

CHAPTER 1: TRANSITIONING THROUGH TEAMING 1

CHAPTER 2: STUDENT-CENTERED TEAM COMMON PLANNING PERIOD (TEAM
            PLANNING)..10

CHAPTER 3: STANDARDIZED EXPECTATIONS..19

CHAPTER 4: CLASSROOM LEADERSHIP 25

CHAPTER 5: LEARNING SKILLS..32

CHAPTER 6: ORGANIZATION AND TIME MANAGEMENT....................................40

CHAPTER 7: PARENT/TEACHER CONTACT 47

CHAPTER 8: TECHNOLOGY 51

CHAPTER 9: STUDENT RECOGNITION...55

CHAPTER 10: SUPPORT SERVICES 60

CHAPTER 11: ORGANIZING YOUR TEAMS: ALL THE SAME BUT VERY DIFFERENT.
            67

CHAPTER 12: YOU GOTTA BELIEVE..80

CHAPTER 13: CLOSING THOUGHTS..94

About the Authors..97

References 99

Preface

We believe that teachers hold tremendous power in their hands. Some have said that teaching is a calling, second only to ministry. We believe that teaching is ministry. We believe that one caring teacher can make all the difference in the life of a young person. This book is for those teachers and educators in the trenches making it happen and fighting the battles everyday. We hope to offer you a little more ammunition to help you do your job. We believe you are worth it and, most importantly, that every single child in your classroom and in your school is worth it.

This book is about turning freshmen into high school students. It is about turning the entire freshman year into a year of transition, and it is about using a teaming approach to do so. Teaming four teachers and giving them a common set of students is an essential step toward successfully transitioning freshmen. Few programs play as key a role in your school's overall improvement and growth as the role played by your Freshman Transition Program.

Freshman Transition means more than simply getting students ready to be in high school. Rather, by Freshman Transition we refer to the efforts that a team of teachers and an entire school implement throughout the ninth-grade year to transition freshmen into high school students ready for success.

We want to share with you our ideas about why teaming teachers works with freshmen, how teaming teachers can work, and how teaming teachers benefits a school. We hope that as a result you will either give teaming a serious look or gain new insights into how you can improve your current teaming situation.

More importantly, though, this book is about teaching. We feel strongly that the profession of teaching plays an integral role in the success of both individuals and society. We hope this book will inspire you as you inspire others.

Chapter 1

Transitioning Through Teaming

THE BEST AND THE WORST

"It was the best of times; it was the worst of times."

When Charles Dickens penned those famous words, he was referring to the infamous French Revolution; however, he could just as easily have been describing the typical ninth-grade year.

Do you remember your ninth-grade year? If you do, you probably understand what we are talking about. On the one hand, ninth grade and high school can be the best of times. You have finally moved past middle school and on to the more exciting high school. Socially, you receive more freedom. There are sporting events to attend, friends to hang out with, and dances that give you a great excuse to ask out a member of the opposite gender. It is as if the previous nine years of school have been simply practice for where you are now. Your whole life is in front of you, and you have been given the chance to begin shaping it. How exciting! These are the best of times.

On the other hand, you are a ninth grader. Full of fear and apprehension, you enter the high school. Middle school somehow seemed safer, almost an extension of the nurturing elementary school where the teacher gave you a hug everyday. You will not admit it, but you miss that. You are full of questions. Will the seniors initiate you? Will you get lost? What group will you fit into? Ninth grade is full of awkwardness. If you are a boy, then most of the girls in your grade consider you too immature to date. You know they are right, but it is hard all the same. If you are a girl, you likely are experiencing pressure that you never knew existed. Fitting in is so important, but with whom should you fit in? Ninth grade, what a time of confusion! Are you still a child, or is it time to be a more serious young adult? The future seems so far away, yet everyone is talking to you about it. You feel like you should have more freedom, and yet at the same time, whenever you have freedom, you seem to blow it. The high school is challenging. These seem like the worst of times.

If you think back to your ninth-grade year, more than likely the majority of your memories will revolve around social issues. That is because social life, friends, and dating dominate the thoughts of the typical ninth grader. In fact, a 1998 study by C.J. Hertzog and L.P. Morgan asked freshmen to rate what was most important to them as they transitioned into high school. The only finding of any significance was that the students were interested in developing close friendships. Yet in this world dominated by social issues, we educators are attempting to lay the academic foundation that will give students the tools necessary to unlock the doors of their future.

Robert Lynn Canady of the University of Virginia's Curry School of Education has dubbed the ninth grade year as the "make it or break it" year. As educators who work with ninth graders, we agree whole-heartedly. Look around your high school. Where are the majority of the problems? Where are the high failure rates, the high discipline and truancy rates? Where are teachers finding themselves the most frustrated and where are students having the least success? What is the one grade in your school that many faculty members believe does not belong in your school? The answer to all of those questions is the ninth grade. Sometimes it seems like ninth grade is simply the "break it" year.

Many reports have verified what ninth grade teachers know from experience. For example, Pittsburgh Public Schools reported that their ninth graders had the worst attendance rate (78%), the worst percentage of failing grades (25.5%), and the worst retention rate (23.4% during the regular school year) of any grade in the school system. On top of all this, 33.8% of ninth graders, just over one in three, were suspended during the ninth-grade year (Chute, 1999).

C.J. Hertzog and L.P. Morgan (1997) reported that ninth-grade retention rates had reached 40% in some schools. According to a recent article in *The Christian Science Monitor*, the rate of ninth-grade retention has tripled in the past thirty years (Jonsson, 2004). This high rate of retention, meaning that large numbers of freshmen must repeat the ninth grade, causes the typical freshman class to stay unnaturally large, an issue that creates additional problems for a school as it tries to provide adequate staffing for its students. The ninth-grade problem is very real.

On the other hand, ninth grade is also the foundation year for most high schools. Ninth grade is the real beginning of the all-important transcript. Ninth grade is when the future begins to become a reality, when students begin to see the road ahead of them and to understand what is required for traveling it. For our students who "make it," ninth grade is the year when the successful habits get the watering and nurturing they require.

Ninth grade also serves a critical role in determining the culture of a school. Where do your students learn what it means to be a part of your school? Where does school spirit or lack thereof begin?

There is no question that throughout the country there is a ninth-grade problem. However, we feel strongly that there is also no question that the ninth grade can be turned into a positive. Rather than being a problem, the ninth grade can serve as an incredible opportunity for both a school and a student. If a school trains its ninth graders in the ways of success, then in four short years the entire atmosphere of a school can be positively altered. In other words, the ninth-grade opportunity can transform a school from the bottom up. Likewise, if a student plays the cards right, ninth grade can pave the way to a tremendous future. By taking the right courses, learning the proper study habits, figuring out how to succeed socially, and by becoming involved properly in their schools, ninth graders can lay a foundation upon which a tremendous house can be built. How important it is that the freshman opportunity is not wasted.

The good news is that it does not have to be wasted. This book will share from our experience working with all types and sizes of schools in turning this problem into an opportunity; however, we are not the only ones having success with ninth graders. Research has shown that while across the country ninth graders have the highest failure rates, those retention rates decrease when transition programs that provide strong social and academic support are in place (McIver, 1990).

Hertzog and Morgan's research in the state of Georgia shows that the more extensive the transition program, the lower the school's dropout and retention rates. In fact, the schools they studied that had only a freshman counselor to assist with registration and/or a building tour for rising ninth graders had the highest rates of dropouts and retention (Hertzog & Morgan, 2001). They found a definite positive relationship between a decrease in retention and dropout rate for both male and female students and the degree of the transition practices utilized (Hertzog & Morgan, 1997).

We will share with you a framework for creating a comprehensive Freshman Transition Program. The framework is based on our own experiences working with ninth graders as well as our experiences helping other schools do the same. In the end, we are confident that this framework will better enable you to seize the opportunity that is the freshman year.

WHY BELIEVING?

Before we go any further, we must state that it has been our experience that the ninth-grade problem is primarily the result of students' attitudes and thoughts about school and about themselves. In short, the ninth-grade problem is a believing problem. Many students have beliefs about life that limit their own potential and that stand in the way of success. The problem of believing will be addressed throughout this book; in fact, we consider it to be our most important topic. We will devote all of chapter 12 to the importance of helping students believe and think in a manner that will lead to success. For now we simply want to point out that all the strategies and ideas in this book are shared for the purpose of empowering teachers to do a more effective job addressing the most important ninth-grade problem of all, the problem of believing.

WHY TEAMING?

Many in education view Freshman Transition as a series of events that occur *before* students enter the ninth grade. These events might include tours of the high school during the eighth-grade year, chances to speak with older students about the realities of high school, or middle-school lessons on the study skills that will be necessary to succeed in high school. In no way would we want to criticize such efforts or activities; however, we do want to point out that these activities alone are not enough to create an effective Freshman Transition Program.

We compare events such as those mentioned in the previous paragraph to pre-marriage counseling. As husbands, this book's authors believe strongly in the importance of wise marriage counseling. We would strongly encourage anyone about to enter the institution of marriage to undergo pre-marriage counseling. However, beyond that we would also encourage people to consider ongoing marriage counseling after the wedding. Getting along as spouses is fairly easy before marriage. Pre-marriage counseling, while important, is just preparation for the real thing. After the vows, couples often find marriage to be more difficult than they imagined before the wedding. For husbands and wives, those first few years of marriage are the foundation for the rest of their lives. It is during those years that most need assistance and advice if they are going to build lasting and loving marriages.

This marriage counseling scenario relates very well to the ninth-grade year. We would advise all middle schools to work to prepare young people for high school, but once a student is actually in the ninth grade, he or she will still be in need of assistance and support. No amount of pre-marriage counseling can truly prepare someone for what they will face once married; and no amount of middle-school activities can truly prepare someone to successfully navigate the pitfalls of high school. The ninth-grade year, like the first years of marriage, is the foundation. It must be properly laid.

Therefore, when we discuss Freshman Transition, we are referring to using the entire ninth-grade year to transition young people into being successful high school students. We want them to be successful in the ninth grade, but more importantly, we want them to build the habits and outlooks necessary to be successful beyond the ninth grade and into the future. Accomplishing this task is difficult and requires, in our view, a team approach.

Individual teachers have always worked diligently to prepare their students for success in life. But what we have found is that when teachers work together, they are more effective at achieving their goals. This is why teaming works. It works because it empowers teachers. Any attempt at high school reform or school improvement must focus, first and foremost, on ways to strengthen the teacher's ability to have an impact in the classroom. A team of teachers sharing students and sharing a vision can turn the ninth-grade year into a successful year of transition more effectively than individual teachers working to achieve the same goal on their own.

The word "teaming" means different things to different people, and before we go any further we want to ensure that we are all envisioning the same idea of a team. This will just be a short bulleted list, but each bullet will be discussed in more detail throughout the book. Our concept of teaming looks like this:

- A team consists of four teachers from the four core areas, but interdisciplinary instruction, while a potential bonus, is not the focus. (A team might consist of teachers from other content areas if a school's master schedule can make that happen. However, due to the constraints that teaming teachers places on a master schedule, the four core areas are usually the best place to start.)
- A common team planning time, in addition to an unencumbered personal planning period, is shared by the teachers on the team.
- The students on the teams are mixed heterogeneously or randomly to prevent the creation of a weak team.
- The teams target as much of the freshman population as possible rather than a small select group of freshmen.
- The teams do not need to be physically isolated from the rest of the building, although they can be if so desired and if the physical layout of the building allows it.

• Transition skills and strategies are taught in all of the teamed classes rather than in an isolated transition or study skills period.

This model of teaming to transition freshmen is effective because it empowers teachers to meet the needs of students and because it is adaptable to any setting and any master schedule. We have seen such a model work in large urban settings, small rural settings, upper-middle-class suburbs, and schools that serve populations in poverty. It can work on traditional schedules, four by four blocks, alternating blocks, and any other type of schedule that a school might use. Teaming costs a school very little but offers it a lot. It is a model than can be flexible and that can be adjusted from year to year as the needs of a school and its students change. It is a model that works, and our hope is that by the end of this book you will have discovered ways that it can work for you and your school.

PROFESSIONAL GROWTH FROM TEAMING

Perhaps the most powerful aspect of teaming, and the reason it is such a solid tool for transitioning ninth graders, is the impact it has on the teachers involved. So often we educators exist on our own private islands. We spend an entire day as the only adult within the four walls of our classroom. Occasionally we have hurried discussions with our colleagues in the teachers' lounge or in the hall while we are on bathroom duty. For the most part, though, it is just us and the children. We enter the classroom as new teachers, inexperienced and with a limited skill set. Then, through trial and error, we develop our style and strategies. Along the way we get occasional advice from our co-workers, but usually we must seek it out. We are often afraid to admit that we do not have all the answers. After all, we are supposed to be the omniscient kings and queens of our classroom fiefdoms.

As educators, we are constantly growing and evolving, or at least we should be. Good teachers know their limitations and then look for assistance in overcoming them. Good teachers spend time getting better and seek ways to be more effective. However, in our schools this sort of professional development rarely occurs. Life, the classroom, and our difficult jobs make our days hectic. When we get a chance to speak to an actual adult, we want relief from our work, not a chance to reflect on it. As a result, many teachers stumble into a style that becomes their routine. Do they know they are teaching in the best possible manner? No, but they know they have developed a means to exist and survive. Teaching, though, is about far more than existing and surviving. Teaching is being able to inspire. Teaching is about taking kids on a journey that will open the doors of their futures and equip them to succeed. The measure of effective teaching is not survival; it is student learning.

We do not mean to sound utopian. We are not here to say that teaming is perfect. However, teaming, when done correctly, serves as a powerful source of teacher development. Imagine having a daily team planning period with three other competent adults. Imagine daily being able to engage in discussions that make your day less stressful while at the same time causing you to grow as a professional. Imagine having a support group within your school. This is teaming. As a result, teamed teachers have more opportunities for professional growth and, therefore, a better chance of more quickly developing into stronger teachers.

We have seen countless teachers, at schools we have worked with over the years, benefit from being on a team. We have witnessed non-teamed teachers struggle on their own alone, but then begin to flourish when they are in the professionally enriching environment of a team. We have seen teachers with classroom management weaknesses gain confidence in the ability to enforce rules because they know that they are not the only teachers doing so. They feel the strength that comes from a team, and as a result, are stronger.

Personal Voices

I came into this career having rarely been in a classroom with students of the type that I was to be teaching. For me, while I did not always enjoy everything about school, school was a place in which I could thrive. I saw my education as the key to my future, so I put my all into it. I took rigorous classes, made good grades, was involved with my school, and did well.

Then I became a teacher. For the first time in my life, I was spending considerable amounts of time with students that lacked goals, motivation, and learning skills. My basic philosophy at the time was that individuals should pull themselves up by their own bootstraps. That was the example I had seen growing up. That outlook had served me well in life. Why many of my students didn't see things that way was a mystery to me.

Thank goodness that as a first-year teacher I was placed on a Freshman Transition Team with one of this book's other authors, Ray Moore. From daily discussions with Ray and the other teachers on our team, I gained a new perspective. I realized I was right and wrong in my outlook on life. I was correct that pulling yourself up by your own bootstraps is the attitude that people need to have to be successful. After all, pulling yourself up implies autonomy, self-reliance, confidence, and goal setting. However, my error lay in thinking that all students had the skills necessary to do the pulling. My error was in not realizing my role in teaching them how to pull and why to pull. From Ray, I learned the value of demonstrating how to pull up the boots, of inspiring students to want to pull up the boots, of helping the students pull the boots on the first few times, and of sometimes requiring them to pull them on whether they wanted to or not. This attitude, this belief set, and this outlook is what separates those who merely teach a subject from those who inspire students to become more than they otherwise would. I am a more effective and dynamic teacher because I have been part of a team.

—Scott Habeeb

High school freshmen need help. Teaming is a great way to provide that help; therefore, you desire to know how to create a team. There is no one right way; however, there are certain components to a Freshman Transition Program that we have found imperative for success. Chapters 2 through 10 will highlight these key elements. The graphic organizer you see in Figure 1a will serve as a guideline for the next nine chapters, with each chapter focusing on a different bubble. In each chapter we will explain to you why the bubble's title is so important, describe exactly what we mean by the title of the bubble, and then share with you some practical ways to implement that topic in your own program.

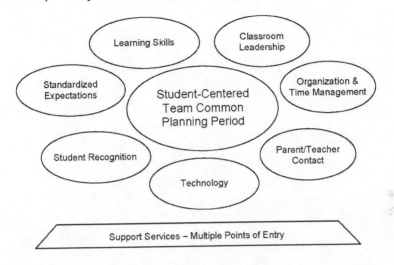

Figure 1a. The above diagram represents the key elements of a successful Freshman Transition Program.

We do not think that the way for you to have success is to do things exactly as we have done. However, we hope you will learn from our ideas and find many that you can put into practice right away. Remember, we have been developing these ideas over the course of fifteen years in many schools. There is no way for a team of teachers to do everything at once, but we hope to give you a road map that will help you build your teams over the years.

We will start with the most important bubble of them all. Right in the middle of the graphic organizer is Student-Centered Team Common Planning. As you will see in this upcoming chapter, this bubble is the reason all the rest are able to exist.

Chapter 2

Student-Centered Team Common Planning Period (Team Planning)

WHY TEAM PLANNING?

Imagine a high school football team that only meets on Fridays ten minutes before kick-off. No practice. No running the same plays over and over again until they're perfect. No watching film. No "go get 'em" speeches from the coach. No sweating together in August to build the bonds necessary to win together in November. It would truly be a disaster. In fact, it would be hard to call it a team.

Now imagine being a team of teachers without team planning. You meet together in the summer to discuss teaming. Then school starts and you go your separate ways. Periodically you happen to bump into each other and discuss what is going on in class. Maybe your rooms are near each other so between class periods you share the sighs of exasperation so common in our profession. Perhaps you even meet after school for a few days to plan an interdisciplinary project. But by and large you are individuals in reality and a team in name only.

Just like the football team that did not practice, the team of teachers would be a disaster. The individual teachers may possess all the requisite skills for having a great school year, and their classrooms may be exciting energetic places of learning. Individually the players might be excellent, but a team is not about individuals.

A team is what you get when you take a number of individuals, combine their talents, and create something that is stronger than the sum of its parts. A team is about synergy, cohesiveness, and the strength of one becoming the strength of all. A team is about a group causing the individuals to be better than they ever could have been on their own. The great coach is the one that can get kids to forget about "I" and "me" and instead become a part of "we". The end result is that "we" do things "I" and "me" could only dream about. That is a team, both on the field and within a school.

In 2003, the Principal's Partnership reported that in studying teaming both at the high-school and middle-school level, the most important factors determining whether or not the team would have a positive impact on student achievement was whether or not the team had enough common planning time and how well the team learned to work together (Muir, 2003). Effective team planning time is the lifeblood of teaming.

So what does a football team do to become a team rather than a collection of individuals? For starters, they begin lifting weights and running *together* in the off-season. They encourage each other to push themselves to the brink, and as a result, they grow physically and bond *together*. Then, about a month before they even play a game, the members of the team begin practicing *together*. For hours in the hot sun they run, hit, sweat, and learn skills— always *together*. They will run the same play or practice the same drill over and over until they finally get it right and are all on the same page. Once the season starts, things pick up even more. The team watches film *together* at least once a week. They practice *together* everyday after school. The night before a game they go out to eat *together* and begin to help each other become mentally prepared for the game. On game day, whether by wearing their jerseys or by wearing a shirt and tie, the members of the team will all dress alike. They give high fives in the hallway and talk *together* about the victory they'll be experiencing *together* that night. Finally game time arrives. Onto the field marches a team, bonded by hard work and most importantly by the feeling of *together*ness that has developed. They are ready for success.

If there were one word that summed up what made that team a team, it would have to be "together." They did things together and as a result were able to become stronger than they were individually. If a team of teachers is going to have the same successful outcome, if the team is going to become stronger than the sum of its parts, then the team must have togetherness as well. The way to create this is through regular team planning time.

A student-centered team common planning period is the centerpiece of teaming. In our travels, we have encountered schools where they have tried to team, but have not given their teachers that regular team-planning period. These schools report back that teaming made little impact. The obvious reason for the lack of success is that these schools did not actually have teams of teachers any more than the football players who do not practice together are a team. Teaming without team planning is not team teaching.

Administrators must make giving teachers time to meet together, preferably daily, a priority. This time should not be in place of a personal planning period (although it is not unreasonable for block teachers who have 90 minutes for personal planning to use the first 30–45 minutes for team planning). Providing time for team planning means that teachers are not available for other purposes. They will not be able to keep a study hall, be on lunch duty, or help out in the attendance office. However, that relatively small sacrifice will reap huge rewards in the future.

Teachers must realize that the time they have been given is precious. The school could have them doing any number of other duties. That time is also an opportunity for professional growth at a rate probably never before seen. Teachers must take advantage of the gift of team planning.

If you were told that if you could give someone five dollars a day and would at the end of the month receive $1,000 in return, would you do it? Or would you just worry about the fact that you were "losing" five dollars each day? This is called "missing the forest for the trees." Teachers, if you were told that you could sacrifice some time each day when you could be grading papers or making copies and the result would be an opportunity to impact students like never before, would you do it? If your answer is no, then you have "missed the forest for the trees." You have traded becoming the best teacher you could be for being able to grade papers and make copies.

Team planning leads to enhanced effectiveness in the classroom, just as team practice makes a quarterback more effective on the field. As teachers, we ought not trade effectiveness for anything. As effective teachers we do more than just enjoy our jobs. We touch lives, change futures, and inspire. Being part of a dynamic team will better enable you to do that. But for the team to be a team, there must be togetherness; there must be team planning

WHAT HAPPENS IN TEAM PLANNING?

In answer to the question of what happens in team planning, we like to say that "it" happens in team planning. By "it" we mean a little bit of anything and everything. As you read this book you may be struck by the number of programs, ideas, and activities that we are advocating as necessary for transforming your ninth grade problem into your ninth grade opportunity.

You may begin to wonder, "How can I ever have the time to do all of that? I am so busy already." The answer to your question is team planning.

Team planning provides a place and a time for the creation of your program. Successful teams are really more of a process than a program. In other words, Day 1 of your team will probably look very different from Day 150 of your team. Furthermore, Day 1,050 might barely resemble Day 200. Every year you will have a different group of students with a different collective personality. From year to year, different teachers will make up your team. Therefore, what worked one year might not work the next. New ideas and plans might need implementation to meet the needs of the teachers and students on your team. If your teams are static, they will be unable to bend and change as necessary. If instead you have put into place a dynamic process, you will be able to evolve to face each new challenge. This evolution and change will only be able to occur if the teachers on the team are regularly meeting to discuss their students and classes. Team planning provides the opportunity to make the static dynamic and to meet the needs of students.

One of the great benefits of team planning is the opportunity for teachers to share ideas and have their own professional in-service sessions. A combination of four teachers has a collective knowledge base and skill set that will enable it to conquer almost any problem it faces in a school. Often, though, teachers exist on their own island. Sometimes they stumble into solutions. However, they often simply get better at doing what they already do. If what they already do is not good enough, if what they already do is not what is necessary to solve a classroom problem, then there are few opportunities to gain new perspectives. While teachers talk in the teacher's lounge and department offices, those hurried conversations between classes or during a short lunch period rarely lead to a solution. More often than not, such conversations become "gripe sessions" that actually have a negative impact on the teacher's ability to grow professionally.

What teachers need is an organized and regular opportunity to share strategies and ideas with other professionals. Team planning provides this. Teachers who use team planning properly will quickly see their skill set grow. For example, perhaps there is a teacher on the team who is an expert on using the Internet to bolster student learning. His strength can become the strength of the rest of the team as he shares his ideas. Perhaps another teacher on the team has no classroom management problems at all. She can share her strategies with a younger member of the team who needs help. Maybe another teacher on the team is an expert at fun review games. Pretty soon the other team members will be able to create exciting review activities of their own.

Team planning allows team teachers to create these symbiotic and professionally enhancing relationships. Teachers benefit by being able to do their jobs more effectively, which in turn benefits students who now have even better teachers. But the benefits of the relationships that form through team planning will not end there. As the team teachers grow professionally, their growth will have a positive effect on the entire school climate. Effective administrators will have these teachers share their new strategies on school-wide in-service days. Teachers of upper grades will be able to utilize many of the same ideas with their students. The time invested in team planning provides dividends that cause the entire school to be positively affected.

Personal Voices

One of Ray's greatest strengths lies in his ability to understand typical ninth graders. As a brand new teacher, I did not. Ray was aware of this and used time in team planning to have discussions about our students. During these discussions I began to gain insight into whom I was teaching. Without this team planning time, I feel I might either have taken much longer to realize what makes my students tick, or I would have instead developed negative attitudes and views toward the immaturities that go hand-in-hand with being a fifteen year old. Because of the sharing of ideas that went on between Ray and me, I instead began to be able to understand my students, and as a result, love them the way they need to be loved.

I was a young teacher. Ray was an experienced veteran. It is easy to see how I benefited from being with him in team planning. However, Ray will tell you that he benefited from the relationship as well. Contrary to popular belief, you can teach an old dog new tricks. Two "tricks" I knew were how to create a Web site and how to use PowerPoint. In team planning we had time to work together as a group practicing these skills. As a result, every teacher on our team ended up creating his or her own Web site filled with resources for their students, and every teacher on our team began using PowerPoint as a way to enhance what was already happening in the classroom.

—Scott Habeeb

CONFERENCES AND MEETINGS

Because the time allotted for team planning is an investment made by the school, it is imperative that the team teachers keep track of what they accomplish with that investment. Look for ways to show that you have been a good steward of your school's resources. At the end of your first year of teaming, ask to make a presentation to your local school board. Share with the board the amazing things you have been doing as a team. Help them see that their investment is not only worthwhile, but also worth continuing. To do this effectively you will need to have kept some data. Perhaps the easiest data to track, as well as the data that makes the most compelling argument for the usefulness of team planning, is conferencing data.

Team planning provides a wonderful opportunity for professional conferencing of all types. One of the best uses of team planning is for meeting with parents. In today's world, because more and more parents work and because so many are single parents, it is very difficult for the typical parent to find the time to meet with his or her child's teachers. However, a team of teachers that has a regular team planning period can tell a parent that they can meet at 10:00 AM (or whenever their team planning period is) any day the parent wants. This convenience means that not only can the parent meet on any day of his choosing, but he also gets to meet with four teachers at once. Teachers will appreciate the fact that team planning reduces the number of before and after school conferences and eliminates the potential of meeting alone with an angry parent.

Team planning should be used to meet with students as well. There is always a student with whom to meet. Someone needs encouragement, someone needs a reality check, or someone needs to be reminded of the team's expectations. If a team so desired, they could meet with a different student every day of the week and at the end of the year still not have met with enough.

Keep in mind that the students you meet with during team planning time are coming from other teachers' classrooms. Since the students' core area teachers are all in team planning together, you will probably be getting students out of study halls, foreign language classes, electives, or physical education classes. Your team needs to make efforts to not interrupt the same teacher's class too often. Also, at the beginning of each year, it would be wise to explain to the other teachers exactly why you might need to pull students out occasionally. Finally, it is a polite practice to try not to pull students out without giving some advance warning to the teachers involved. You may even want to give the other teachers a choice of days and let them select when it would be most convenient for them to lose a student for a few minutes and invite them to share concerns that they have for the team to address.

Here is an idea of a way to use team planning to meet with students that can really impact your school year positively. After a couple of days of school, begin discussing your students. As a team, compile a list of all the students that fit into any of the following three categories: students who might have difficulty academically, students who might have difficulty behaviorally, and quiet students who could "fall through the cracks" or be difficult to get to know in a classroom full of students. Divide your list in half. Have half of the team teachers meet with one half of the list and the other half of the team teachers meet with the other half. Then begin scheduling ten-minute "get to know you" conferences during your team planning periods. Each pair of team teachers can probably meet with four students in a planning period. If the team does this twice a week, in the first six weeks of school it can meet with almost one hundred students.

What a great way to start off the year—having a non-confrontational, friendly conference before confrontation ever becomes necessary. Spending ten minutes asking a child "What did you do this weekend?" or "What's your favorite movie?" is an easy yet powerful way to let a child know that you are interested in her, that you care about who she is as a person, and that you are more than a teacher—you are a human being.

Personal Voices

I'll never forget one such meeting with a young lady who frankly intimidated me a little. She didn't smile; in fact, she scowled. She wore dark make-up and dark shirts and exuded an attitude that basically said, "Leave me alone." It would have been tempting to do just that. If our team had simply not bothered her, she probably would have not bothered us. Have you ever had that sort of tacit agreement with a student?

I wondered how our meeting with her would go. Our first question to her was "What's your favorite movie?" My jaw almost hit the floor when she replied, "*The Little Mermaid*." Come to find out, inside that gruff exterior and beneath that angry shell, lived a little girl who loved Disney movies. Immediately, I realized that my first impression had been incomplete. What if we hadn't met with her? What if we hadn't taken a little time to get to know her? I might have given up on her before actually giving her the chance she deserved. This creative use of the team planning period enabled us to better meet that young lady's needs, as well the needs of numerous other students, in a more appropriate and more effective manner than we otherwise would have.

—Scott Habeeb

A team planning period also provides a wonderful opportunity to meet with other professionals in your building and in your system. Administrators and guidance counselors should make a point to stop by the teams once a week. This will allow them to stay in tune with the needs of the teams and to support the teams so that their impact on the school is maximized. Along with administrator and counselor meetings, team teachers can also use their team-planning period as a time to schedule meetings for special discipline circumstances, meetings with school nurses and psychologists, and meetings to deal with special education concerns.

Keep track of these meetings. Have all your teams work together to make a plan for how to keep this data. You will begin to see what an incredible resource team planning is for teachers. Then share that data with others so they will see that as well.

KEEPING THE FLAME ALIVE

When teachers on a team use their team-planning period to inspire one another and keep each other focused on the goal, they elevate team planning to an entirely new level. So often, we in education are battered about by the waves so much that we decide to keep our boat at the dock. We have a tendency to forget the incredible destination toward which we are sailing. Furthermore, we forget that the waves do not have to batter us. Instead, if we know how to navigate them, the ride can be breathtaking.

It is important for members of a team to understand that a certain amount of venting should be allowed in team planning when necessary. If we are not able to let off steam, sometimes we will pop. Venting in team planning can prevent the popping; however, the venting should have a constructive outcome. As a team, make a commitment to let each other vent about a child, but to then bring the discussion of the child either to a discussion of positive attributes of the student or to possible solutions to whatever the problem is. Team planning must never become the stereotypical teacher's lounge where students are put down. A constructive outcome is necessary, so that the venting will not need to last beyond team planning.

Think of it as a family. The teachers are the parents, and the students are the children. Sometimes a husband and wife will vent about their children. However, they do not tell the whole world about their frustrations. That is family business. Furthermore, their discussions of the shortcomings of their children usually end in a new plan for helping the children overcome their areas of weakness. This is how it should work in team planning.

Team planning helps teachers keep their sanity. It enables them to keep the big picture in mind. Teachers often go through their entire day without meaningful and positive adult interaction. Team teachers with team planning do not have that problem. They have the privilege of meeting daily with other professionals all dedicated to the same goal. As a result, the odds of focusing on and fearing the waves, and therefore staying at the dock, grow slimmer. The odds of enjoying the sail increase with every constructive team-planning period.

As educators, we also can inspire one another. We can share successes, strategies, and ideas that spur one another on. We can keep, alive and strong in our fellow educators, the flame that was lit when we decided to go into teaching.

Team planning—do not try to be a team without it.

Personal Voices

I remember a team-planning period during the spring of my second year of teaching. It was that time of year when everyone is tired, vacation seems forever away, and the kids act as though they are being fed nothing but pure sugar. That day in team planning we were, to say the least, venting about our students. We were all very frustrated with our students. After a while, Ray made a profound statement that has stayed with me to this day. He said, "Let's not forget that the things that often drive us the craziest about these kids are also the same things that often make us love them the most." The incredible truth of the statement immediately changed my attitude. I had been frustrated because my students were rambunctious, hyper, and immature. Ray's statement turned my frustrations around 180 degrees. The truth is, I love my students because they have energy, are full of life, and have such youthful spirits.

I went back to my next class period with a new perspective. The bell rang for class to start and it happened. One of my students, who we will call James and who had a propensity for disruption and trouble, had a straw down his shirt. He was blowing air into his large armpit and creating a very flatulent sound. I'm convinced that if he had done that prior to team planning that day, I would have nailed him. Instead I looked at him and thought, "What energy! What youth! I love this kid."

When I called his name out, he knew he was in trouble. I asked him to bring his straw up to the front of the room. He slowly made his way to where I stood, awaiting yet another punishment from another teacher. You should have seen the surprise in his eyes when I said, "James, that is hilarious. Would you do that for the whole class?"

It took him a moment to realize that I was serious, and then he blew that straw like a champ! The whole class laughed, and then we proceeded with the day's lesson.

—Scott Habeeb

Chapter 3

Standardized Expectations

RESPONSIBILITY IS THE CONTENT

Would you test something before you taught it? We are not referring to pre-tests or other creative assessments designed to activate prior learning. If you had fallen behind on your pacing guide, would you ever consider handing out a few unit tests, grading them, and moving on? The mere thought of doing so is preposterous. Teachers teach so that students will learn, and then we assess and hopefully re-teach if necessary. Yet students routinely receive grades that not only reflect their learning, but how responsible, or irresponsible, they may happen to be. Most teachers, if they are honest with themselves, can easily recognize that much of a student's grade is a measure not only of content but also of responsibility.

Think of all the highly capable students who, when engaged in conversation about content, convey that they possess not only the facts but also demonstrate the ability to draw connections, make inferences, and apply content at a higher level, but because of missing assignments, incomplete work, or a failure to prepare for formal assessments, earn lower grades than other students. Other students may have a lesser grasp of the material, but faithfully complete every assignment and have good study habits. They may rarely get the big picture or construct their own understanding that will provide the necessary foundation for future use of the content. Odds are good that you have known many students like this and have observed that being prepared for class, paying attention, faithfully completing assignments, studying for tests, and generally being responsible frequently lead to better grades than being irresponsible. If it is true that grading practices frequently assess a student's level of responsibility, then we need to teach responsibility before we grade it.

Issues of responsibility often act as roadblocks, pitfalls, and landmines for students in our schools. Test grades likely reflect more than just content knowledge. They also reflect whether or not the student studied, or if the student even has a time and place for studying. They reflect whether or not the student possesses the time management skills necessary to recognize that there is a test coming and that time to study needs to be scheduled into the student's busy life. If a student's grade in a course is likely going to include some function of how responsible the student is, it stands to reason that we ought to teach responsibility before we grade it—especially if we are going to help ninth graders transition into high school.

THE POWER OF 4 (TEACHERS⁴)

What if you had between four and eight supervisors each day, and every time a bell rang your supervisor changed and so did the expectations for your performance. For 45–90 minutes, you are the model employee, you receive praise, and you accomplish much. Suddenly, a tone sounds and a new supervisor enters who expects you to do things differently and reprimands you when, out of routine, you perform your job like you did just moments ago. You grit your teeth and bite your tongue because you know that in time the tone will sound again and you will be free of this boss and begin dealing with the next. In a very short time, you would likely suffer from low job satisfaction and not be a very productive employee. Other employees lack the capacity to grin and bear it, so they quit or become contentious and get fired.

In many schools, the above scenario is a perfect description of what the typical ninth grader experiences upon entering the high school. We have heard teachers complain many times that ninth graders have trouble keeping up with what is expected of them. Perhaps part of the problem lies in the expectations.

One of the simplest and most powerful steps that a team of teachers responsible for transitioning freshmen into high school can take is to standardize their expectations. It matters little what the expectations are, just that they are standardized. For the students, they no longer have to go through thought processes like the following:

"I am in science now where we get to sit wherever we want and don't have to copy the question if we integrate the question into our answer, but also where I must never be caught with a piece of gum."

And then, "I sure am glad I was on time for history because here one tardy results in detention, but at least we can chew gum. I better not forget, though, that I need to write the question before I answer it."

For teachers, standardizing expectations dramatically increases compliance and results in less time wasted on restating routine and more time on teaching and learning. For students, the guesswork is relieved and routine is quickly established. Moving from class to class still involves a different teacher and subject matter, but the expectations are consistent. Most students are relatively polite and will do what is asked of them as long as they know what is being asked. If classroom rules are like ever-shifting sand, we unintentionally convey to students a message that says, "There are so many different expectations during the day that you will never keep up with all of them, so why bother with any of them?"

On the contrary, when students know what is expected and generally comply with our expectations, we are able to enjoy teaching the subjects we love without wasting so much time and energy on the mundane, everyday tasks associated with running a classroom.

Personal Voices

When I was in the ninth grade, I had German 2 immediately before Bluebird English 9. OK, it wasn't really called *Bluebird* English 9, but now that I am an educator, I know that it was not a heterogeneous group of students. Most of us were relatively bright, motivated, and college bound, so we were in a course with a teacher who really taught us to write. We wrote a lot and learned to write well. Regrettably, my grades seldom accurately reflected how well I could write because I frequently lost points for failing to use college-ruled notebook paper, crowding a margin, failing to leave the last two lines blank for teacher feedback, or using an incorrect heading on my paper. You see, in the class period before Bluebird English 9, I was in German 2 with a teacher who expected us to use a three-line header in the upper left-hand corner of the paper that featured our German names on the first line, the date (in the European sequence of day, month, year) on line two, and our class period on line three. In English for Bluebirds, however, we were expected to use a three-line header in the upper right-hand corner with our class period on line two, and the date on line three. If this essential information was in the wrong place on the paper or the lines were in the wrong order, there was a penalty in both classes. In the worst-case scenario, you would use the European date format on an English assignment and lose a bunch of points because 14/5/81 wasn't a real date in a world with only twelve months in a year!

A year or two later, I had a science class where any assignment, homework, lab, or test that was turned in without a name written on it was graded as a zero. Interestingly enough, the teacher was able to determine who to assign the zero to in the grade book. According to school legend, a student in a previous year had begun just turning in sheets of paper with his name on the top and argued that if failing to write his name resulted in a zero then successfully writing his name should result in a 100% "A." Sound reasoning in the opinion of my peers!

—Alan Seibert

STANDARDIZED EXPECTATIONS SHOULD BE HIGH EXPECTATIONS

Making things less confusing for students and more pleasant for teachers is likely reason enough to begin standardizing right away, but it is just a beginning. The real boost to student achievement occurs when a team of teachers makes the expectations instructionally relevant and very high. Imagine if you were the only teacher in the ninth grade who used a seating chart, assigned homework every night, even on weekends, and had a strong and consistent policy for late work. What if you were the only teacher who required students to be in their seat and already working on a "Do Now" assignment before the tardy tone, required a research-based note taking system, insisted on higher-order thinking in all assignments, and never permitted students to pack up early, put their heads down, or waste even a minute of instructional time? On the buses and in the lunchroom, you would likely be referred to as the unrealistic jerk.

When a team of teachers share these same, seemingly unrealistically high expectations for all students, most students fall in line. Instead of any one teacher being "the jerk" for expecting so much, high expectations become just the way things are done. With consistent high expectations reinforced daily by a team of teachers, relatively immature freshmen can be transformed into high school students capable of success.

SOUNDS GREAT ... WHAT'S THE CATCH?

You may be wondering why more teachers do not use standardized expectations if they can be so powerful, or why entire schools do not standardize all expectations. Even though clear and consistently enforced expectations can quickly improve student conduct and learning for an entire school, getting four or more teachers to first agree on a set of expectations and then to enforce them consistently is a significant undertaking. Most all teachers have their preferred way of doing things. Invariably, it is the process of standardizing expectations that requires the most time and effort during our work with schools seeking to establish a Freshman Transition Program, but it is effort well invested. When done right, the process helps all teachers build a sense of camaraderie, and puts in place a foundation that enables more students to achieve at a higher level.

We recommend that team teachers meet during the summer before each school year to discuss their expectations. Remember, your team make-up will be dynamic, with teachers coming and going from the teams most years. Therefore, it is essential to make sure you start off each year on the same page. During this summer meeting, the teams must reach consensus on what their expectations will be. Then they must pledge to stick to those expectations and support them during the upcoming school year. Teachers who decide during the school year that they do not like a specific expectation need to be reminded that they have agreed to support the teams in this area for the year, but that they can bring up the idea of changing things during the next summer.

When teams meet in the summer to discuss expectations, we recommend that each team create three categories of potential expectations and techniques to be used by the teams. The three categories are:

1. Expectations that are standardized for ALL of the grade-level teams. An example of this that we recommend is for students to have homework every night. This makes it much easier for parents to know if there is homework since there is always homework. It might not be much, it may have been finished in school, and it might not be graded, but there is always something that needs to be done. Imagine, though, if one team had this expectation and another team did not. Parents and students would perceive one team as easy and the other as hard.

2. Expectations that are standardized for a team of teachers but not necessarily all teams. An example of this might be the use of seating charts. While we think all teachers should use these (more to come in chapter 4), if one team did not, it would not necessarily hurt a team that did.

3.   <u>Expectations that remain teacher-specific.</u> An example of this would be using a night light during the use of video clips. There is really no need to make this a team policy.

Once the teams have divided their ideas into these three categories, they should then compare lists. In doing so, they must ensure that everything in the first category is agreed upon.

It is difficult to overstate the importance and effectiveness of standardizing expectations for students, but it matters little how clear the message is or even how well-crafted the standardized expectations are if our classrooms lack the leadership necessary to ensure that students meet or exceed the expectations. Without teaching responsibility, giving students examples to follow, and providing opportunities to practice the desired skills, standardized expectations can become little more than a universally applied means of proving that most students are inclined to be irresponsible and then penalizing them for it.

Freshmen have a lot to manage when they come to high school. Unfortunately, many of them are unable to do so very well. But a team of teachers that standardizes its expectations can remove many of the unnecessary barriers that prevent students from finding success. Furthermore, these standards, if they are sufficiently high and consistently enforced, can help our freshmen reach heights never before thought possible.

Personal Voices

Early in my career, another teacher chided my efforts to help students by saying, "Alan, you can lead a horse to water but you can't make him drink." Being too young and inexperienced to recognize the informal power that some veteran teachers possess, I retorted, "Well, it is our job to make the horse thirsty!" In the years since, I have heard it said much better with sayings such as, "Good teachers salt the oats" or "Good teachers serve crackers." The point remains the same, though, that it is up to the teacher to create a culture in which learning can occur!

—Alan Seibert

Chapter 4

Classroom Leadership

Effective management without effective leadership is like straightening the deck chairs on the Titanic.

—*Stephen Covey*

In your teacher preparation program, you likely spent some time in your methods coursework on classroom management, perhaps embedded in your educational psychology class. However, our experience has led us to believe that most people who aspire to our profession are not adequately prepared by the time they are hired to be the leader of the classroom of the students in their charge.

If you have ever been a student or an observer in a class that was lacking classroom management, you will probably remember that it was hectic and stressful on everyone, the teacher probably most of all. In our experience, teachers new to the profession frequently have the most trouble with creating an atmosphere that is conducive to learning. The problem with emphasizing classroom management is that it creates a narrow view of the professional's responsibility in the classroom, suggesting that if you can keep everyone seated and quiet, learning will occur. One of the rewarding aspects of being part of team is using the power of four teachers working together to go beyond mere classroom management and instead help each other become classroom leaders.

If you pause to consider and visualize the Covey quote at the introduction of this chapter, you can easily imagine the scene. Now consider the educational corollary. Can you recall being a student in a classroom where all the desks were in straight rows and the teacher managed the class so well that no one dared to misbehave? In reality, someone on occasion probably did misbehave, but the teacher-dictator hounded the administration to remove the child from the class or, if an elective, encouraged that same student to drop the course, often with bitter sarcasm. In fact, if the teacher-dictator has been harsh enough for a long enough period of time, students will drop without ever entering the room, and administrators in the summer will be tempted to review the class list and reschedule students who are likely not to get along with that teacher. Now reflect on what you learned in the class with a dictator. Odds are good that you remember little from the experience except that it was quiet, nobody said or did much, and little was learned.

As the professional in the classroom, it is not enough for a teacher to manage behavior in an effort to convey knowledge. Effective teachers are educational leaders, who lead students in positive and meaningful learning activities and experiences. In your own experience, the best teachers were probably not the ones who ruled with an iron fist or sought to be every student's new friend. Instead they were the ones that created an environment so engaging that there was seldom a disciplinary problem. The very culture of the classroom precluded most problems from occurring, and when problems did occur, there was sufficient rapport, trust, and respect to resolve the matter quickly and with a positive outcome.

LEADERSHIP STRATEGIES

Individual teachers seeking to become leaders of students rather than enforcers of rules are encouraged to read *Teaching with Love and Logic* by Jim Fay and David Funk (1998). In it, readers learn effective and practical strategies for becoming leaders in their classrooms by establishing an atmosphere of mutual respect, courtesy, and love. Like most aspects of teaching, when teachers work together as a team in a Freshman Transition Program, classroom leadership strategies become easier to implement and more effective, thanks to the power of Standardized Expectations.

As you and your school plan for your transition program, seek to develop strategies, with which all teachers on the team are comfortable, that can be employed to create a positive classroom culture. Do not just hope this happens. Instead, make it happen. Seek to use your combined strengths to create an atmosphere in which your freshmen will best be able to find success. Here are a few ideas that we have found helpful. It is by no means an exhaustive list, and for the most part, the ideas are not new. We hope, though, that our ideas will help you better understand how teachers working as a team can make even simple ideas powerful.

SEATING CHARTS

One tried-and-true classroom leadership technique involves the use of seating charts. Like most techniques, however, if the method is not rooted in a sound rationale and consistently implemented, its usefulness is severely minimized. For example, the teacher who only uses seating charts as a means to help take attendance is missing out.

First and foremost, on the first day of school, a seating chart is a way to convey an assuring and welcoming message to students. It tells students that everyone has a place in the classroom. It also tells students that the teacher is in charge and makes decisions about the structure and organization of the class.

As we have previously discussed, high school freshmen are preoccupied with social matters. Your goal in the classroom, though, is to encourage them to focus on academic matters. A seating chart can help relieve much of the tension that social issues bring to a classroom. For example, boys no longer have to argue about who gets to sit next to the pretty girl. Students left out of cliques that form in the hallways no longer have to feel left out in the classroom. Less confident or shyer individuals know that they do not have to struggle to find their place in the classroom. If a team of teachers can alleviate the impact of these and other social pressures in the classroom, then they can get down to the business of helping their students find the academic success that will carry them throughout high school.

ONE LARGE THREE-RING BINDER

Another straight-forward conventional idea is for a team of teachers to require that students use one, large three-ring binder for all their teamed classes. It helps students keep themselves organized, and makes it easier to know which notebook to bring to class since they only have one. Best of all, for teachers, is that we never need to hear, "I brought the wrong notebook to class."

Few ideas we have used within teams have been this simple, yet few have done more to quickly and easily remove a major stumbling block for freshmen. Whether they do it inadvertently or purposefully, students are often unprepared because they brought the wrong notebook to class. This makes creating a culture of success an extra difficult task. Students who are not prepared cause teachers to either waste time helping them gather materials or to ignore the students' situation and allow them to not keep up with the day's activities. Neither of these alternatives is acceptable.

Do Now Assignments

For years, effective teachers have used Madeline Hunter's anticipatory sets or, as we like to call them, Do Now assignments. This idea is nothing new, but the power lies in a team of teachers using it consistently. Time on task is important in a classroom. Freshmen love to make starting class difficult. The effective teachers who have tried Do Now assignments have had to train students who, in other classrooms, are not required to begin class right when the bell sounds. This does not have to be the case on a team.

A team of teachers can teach freshmen how to start class efficiently and effectively, an important aspect of a classroom culture of success, by requiring that each class begin with a Do Now assignment. Whether it is a quote for students to reflect upon, a sample problem to practice, or an overhead chart created by the textbook company, the point is that in all teamed classes, students are required to begin class immediately.

As previously stated, the lone teacher that has such high expectations of students is often viewed as a jerk. However, when a team of teachers share this expectation, the students know no other way. Therefore, your high expectations become simply the way the school functions. This is the power of four.

The Yellow Sheet

A team of teachers attempting to transition freshmen into the high school must focus on changing the negative behaviors that get in the way of student success. One way to do this is to create a standardized method for recognizing and rewarding the positive behaviors that lead to a positive classroom culture.

The yellow sheet is a simple behavioral modification tool that, in a non-threatening manner, reminds students that certain behaviors are positive and certain behaviors are not. Imagine Pavlov's dogs with a clipboard and yellow paper substituted for the bell. The color of your daily grade clipboard is not that important, but experience indicates that something bright and eye-catching helps. If most students are going to routinely and consistently adhere to a standardized set of expectations, the teacher leader needs to develop or discover an easy to use, non-confrontational method of recording student choices for large numbers of students on a daily basis that can serve as a carrot for encouraging students to make the right choices.

A team of teachers choosing to use a Yellow Sheet or similar technique should select the expectations that they want to emphasize and monitor. Whenever the students do not exhibit these behaviors, the teacher writes on the Yellow Sheet the letter that stands for the behavior being checked. The Yellow Sheet results in a grade. Multiply the number of behaviors checked by the number of days in the grading period. That number is the Yellow Sheet grade. For every mark a student has, take off one point.

Which expectations to include should be determined by the team of teachers. Here are some possible suggestions that in our experience have worked well.

1. "P" for Preparedness. If a student does not have the proper materials in class, then the student receives a "P."

2. "D" for the Do Now. As you are discussing the Do Now, simply pick up the Yellow Sheet as Pavlov would ring his bell. If a student still does not get started, then you might move toward the student, maybe even tapping the Yellow Sheet on the desk. Ultimately, if the student still does not do the work, then a "D" is marked down.

3. "H" for Homework. During the Do Now, a teacher can walk up and down the aisles easily checking to see if homework was done. If not, then an "H" is recorded.

4. "A" for Attention. A student who will not pay attention in class receives an "A."

5. "C" for Classwork. Students are required to do classwork, even if it's getting started on that night's homework. If they do not, then they receive a "C."

If the above expectations were used, then the Yellow Sheet grade would be five points per day multiplied by the number of days in a grading period. In a class that meets daily in a school with six-week grading periods, the Yellow Sheet would be:

5 expectations x 5 days x 6 weeks = 150 possible points

The number of points described above should not be a sticking point for whether a team of teachers adopts such a strategy. Hopefully, your instruction provides for many opportunities for students to learn, practice, and then demonstrate their learning. If you want students to do something, you need to grade it, whether it is small grades for homework, classwork, and quizzes, or larger grades for labs, tests, papers, and presentations. Teachers who have a lot of grades from a variety of assignments tend to have little problem with a 150-point grade from the yellow sheet. However, even if a teacher on the team is not comfortable with 150 points, the weight of the grade can be modified easily. What is most important is that the expectations are standardized and that students are held accountable.

Other teachers are not bothered by the relative weight of the grade, but are concerned that checking for 150 desired student behaviors for 120 students equals 18,000 bits of record keeping. It is important to recognize that you are only recording poor choices, so unless your classes are incredibly unruly, in which case you desperately need this technique, there will be far more good choices than bad ones.

Similarly, the Yellow Sheet cannot be a club for a teacher who is having a bad day. Team teaching helps here, too. If one teacher is misusing the tool, the misuse will become apparent to the team and an opportunity for team building, and professional growth will be available for the next team-planning period.

We have encountered teachers who regard the Yellow Sheet as a phony grade. Most teachers, though, regard themselves as good teachers. If a student spends an entire grading period in a good teacher's class and consistently brings the required materials, makes good use of class time, completes homework every night, pays attention, and completes teacher-designed classwork, then the student is learning. More than likely that student is learning things that will not happen to be on the exam but were important enough for a good teacher to include as part of the class activities. When properly weighted, the small number of points that the Yellow Sheet can raise a student's grade is probably an accurate reflection of the knowledge and skills gained by the student.

Furthermore, to transition freshmen into high school, we must focus on behaviors. It is important to recognize and reward positive behavior. Therefore, you must teach your students that the Yellow Sheet is their friend. By exhibiting positive behaviors, the Yellow Sheet will make tangible the benefits of their actions. By the same token, since the Yellow Sheet is about behavior, it should not lower a child's grade. Typically, though, a student with lots of marks will already have a low grade, so the point is usually moot.

The question of whether or not we should grade behavior is quite legitimate. We firmly believe that grades needs to represent learning, and that student behaviors should be reported as comments, not as grades. In reality, this technique is more about changing than grading student behaviors.

The grade that results is generally a legitimate indicator of student learning because the Yellow Sheet has a high, positive correlation with a student's final average in a course and even on end-of-course assessments.

The point of the Yellow Sheet, the Do Nows, the team binder, and the seating charts is to create a climate and a culture that helps our freshmen. Whatever strategies your team chooses to employ, keep in mind your goal. You want to be leaders in the classroom. You want to harness the power of four as you do so, and you want to teach your freshmen the skills they need to survive and thrive in high school.

Chapter 5

Learning Skills

Picture your lower achieving freshmen. What are the **root causes** of those students' low achievement? While there are certain academic deficiencies that often get in the way of success, a good teacher can usually overcome these. It is our contention that in almost all cases, the root causes of poor student performance have more to do with attitude than they do with ability. Factoring an equation might be a difficult task for a student, but if the student possesses the right attitude, then she has the skills to learn. Therefore, we must find ways in the classroom to address the topic of attitude. The teacher who does so truly teaches learning skills. Teaching about attitude, what we truly mean by learning skills, must be a central part of your school's transition program.

Personal Voices

One question people tend to ask me since I have been teaching so long is: "Are students any different today than they were a generation or so ago?" For a long time, I did not think so. However, I now think that changes in our society may be causing some differences in the young people. One fellow teacher said a few years ago, "It used to be that when I wanted to talk to someone about responsibility, I would call the parent. Now I have to talk to the grandparent." Scott, Alan, and I do not believe that blaming parents or the students themselves is a productive use of time. However,

---

it is important to understand the characteristics of our society that influence our classrooms. Many of us may now find ourselves teaching students who do not approach life the same way we do. As a matter of fact, many of us were never in classes with students like the ones we teach. Our students may not be growing up in families like ours. They may not have the same work ethic we have. Their idea of what strength looks like may be different. The things they value may very well be different. They may have far different belief systems. It is the responsibility of the teacher to help students learn to think and value that which will lead to their own success. Once we are able to do this, teaching content becomes quite easy.

—Ray Moore

Altering students' attitudes is no small task. Often teachers are combating a lifetime of conditioning. However, this learning process becomes far more effective in a team situation where the same learning skills are being taught in all teamed classes. Teaching learning skills becomes even more successful in schools that adopt the idea of transforming their schools from the bottom up. If certain learning skills and attitudes are taught during the freshman year, then teachers of sophomores, juniors, and seniors can benefit by reinforcing these attitudes in their classes as well.

The idea of taking time to teach students about attitude is not widespread in many schools. Many teachers expect students to arrive in class already possessing the learning skills necessary for success. However, teachers may need to change if they are to meet the goals of No Child Left Behind and reach the students who are the most difficult to reach. When teachers expect all students today to exhibit responsibility, they may not be realistic. If the students do not exhibit responsibility or strong attitudes, maybe it is because they were never taught those skills.

If students lack the prerequisite skills in a course, whether it is grammar or the ability to multiply fractions, then the good teacher teaches those skills to the student. It is the same with responsibility and attitude. When teachers find that students do not have the prerequisite attitude, then the teacher must teach attitude.

Great teachers know how to seize the teachable moment. They know how to respond to a comment in class in such a manner as to help all students gain a new and better perspective. However, the freshman problem that is so evident in today's schools begs for more than the random teachable moment. Because attitude plays such a large role in the success or failure of freshmen, teachers of freshmen must actively seek to create teachable moments.

Personal Voices

When I became a father, I had already been teaching for six years. I had enough experience as a teacher at that point to know that most people are their own worst enemy. I knew that people do not fail because they lack ability. They also do not often fail simply because they are lazy. People fail because of all the obstacles that they throw in their own paths. I figured that parenting would be pretty easy because all I needed to do was teach my own children to avoid undermining their own success. I must admit that I found out that parenting was harder than I thought and that helping children avoid those mistakes is not always easy.

—Ray Moore

BELIEFS AND ATTITUDE AS CONTENT

The remainder of this chapter focuses on the beliefs and attitudes that students need in order to be successful and will share ideas for how a teacher can address these in the classroom.

CHOICE NOT CHANCE/S.L.A.N.T.

One of the most important learning skills for students is to realize that they can take control of their own lives. Many at-risk students believe that life is a matter of chance. In other words, they believe that their success depends on factors that for the most part are outside of their control. They may believe that their success is predetermined by their last name or the street or housing project where they live. While educators should not judge students on such factors, teachers are not the only ones making such judgments. One of the characteristics of at-risk students is that they perceive reasons why they will fail and why the odds are stacked against them. They do this in part so they can quit before they start. This enables them to say that they never tried rather than admit that they failed.

The reality, though, is that while the circumstances of our life do play a role in our journey, the ultimate destination is determined first and foremost by our choices. If students are to be successful they must understand that life is about choice, not chance. One way to teach this learning skill is to teach students how to S.L.A.N.T.

Early in the school year ask your students the following question. "If a teacher doesn't like you, is there anything that you can do about it?" The typical answers will offer great insight into the minds of your students. The stronger students tend to say that there are things they can do to change a teacher's attitude toward them. The weaker students tend to say that there is nothing they can do. Weaker students do not understand "how to play the game" and instead see many interactions with adults and other authority figures as tests of their strength. As such, they will choose to posture, perhaps by refusing to work in that teacher's class. Instead of making the situation better, they will actually do things that will make it worse, and then take that as evidence that there is nothing they can do to control their own educational destiny.

After hearing your students' responses, teach them about S.L.A.N.T. S.L.A.N.T. is an acronym. You will find different versions of it in different places. We like to say that it stands for:

S — **S**it up

L — **L**ean forward

A — **A**ct interested

N — **N**od in agreement

T — **T**rack the teacher with your eyes

Demonstrate for your students how to use S.L.A.N.T., making sure they realize that the nod needs to be very subtle. (Otherwise they tend to look like bobble-head dolls.) Explain to your students that by using S.L.A.N.T. they can actually trick teachers into liking them. Do not tell them that they will actually learn more this way, since that takes the fun out of using it. Encourage them to pick a teacher and S.L.A.N.T. him or her for two weeks.

The point of S.L.A.N.T. is that students can control other peoples' perceptions of them. That is power. Once our students begin to understand the power they have over perceptions, they can begin to see that their choices are more important than life's game of chance.

Personal Voices

There is a story about my father that I like to share with my students. Dad was a lawyer and a very aggressive human being. When I was very young, I remember him coming home each night and complaining about his boss. One night he said that he was going to make his boss love him, and he set about to do it. Essentially, he used S.L.A.N.T. on his boss. About a year later, he got a promotion followed quickly by other promotions. Finally, Dad found himself in the position of being the boss of his ex-boss. I ask my students, "What do you think was the first thing my dad did?" Most of them are correct when they say that he fired his former boss. I conclude this discussion by telling students that I am not trying to foster ideas of revenge. I just want them to learn that strong people know they have to

> play the game. Sometimes working and waiting looks like weakness. The truth is that weak people posture, demand, complain, and yell because that is all they have. They do things that look like strength to them. Sadly, that is all they will ever have until they learn to live life more effectively.
>
> —Ray Moore

VICTIM STATEMENTS

Freshmen often speak victim statements. It is difficult to be a speaker of victim statements and also possess the attitude needed for success. A victim statement is a statement that makes the speaker a victim of something other than his own volition. Victim statements are usually true, at least partially. They are different from lies or excuses. The victim statement raises the question of who is in control: the student and his or her choices, or some outside set of circumstances. Freshmen need to be taught to take control of their lives. It is difficult to do this if you perceive yourself to be a victim of circumstances.

For example, when the due date arrives for the year's first paper in an English class, it is not uncommon for a student to tell the teacher that his paper is not ready because his printer ran out of ink. This might very well be true. Everyone has experienced this sort of situation at one point or another. Teachers need to tell these students that while they do believe the story, the student is giving the teacher a victim statement.

"My printer ran out of ink" is a victim statement because the student is saying that the printer is in control. Some students who find their printer out of ink will e-mail the paper to the teacher. They may bring the paper to school on a flash drive and print the paper there. A few students would even go so far as to copy the paper off the monitor by hand when the printer ran out of ink. Students must not allow a hunk of plastic to control their lives. To do so is to allow oneself to become a victim.

Every time students give up control, teachers need to say, "Victim statement!" Students will protest that what they are saying is true. Remind them, though, of what a victim statement is. Within a few weeks, the students themselves start saying, "Victim statement!" Now you know they understand. Now you know they are beginning to understand that the little things they say influence what they believe, and that what they believe influences who they are and what they do. Now you know that they are beginning to understand the dynamics of gaining control of their own lives.

THE ROLE OF FAILURE

In his book *You Can Be President (Or Anything Else)*, Bob Moore (1994) tells the famous story of failure concerning Abraham Lincoln. Abraham Lincoln lost nine of eleven elections, but some people would say he is the best president who ever lived. In many ways, he became the soul and symbol of our nation. That is not bad for a politician who had a miserable .181 batting average in elections.

Many students are afraid to answer questions in class, and they are afraid to try out for extracurricular activities because they are afraid to fail. Teachers must help students learn that we learn from our failures. Students need to understand that failure happens for one of two reasons. Some fail because they do not try. This is unacceptable. Others fail because they tried and fell short. This is not only acceptable, but laudable as well. Failure is a necessary step in success. In fact, students need to understand that if they would like to increase their success rate in life, they will probably need to increase their failure rate.

Students need to hear more and more examples of how others have grown stronger and learned to succeed through their failures. A book like Bob Moore's can be used to help freshmen, who so often are afraid due to their transition into high school, gain the confidence they need to take chances, to work hard, and to succeed.

ZAP: ZEROES AREN'T PERMITTED

Many students do not understand the impact that zeroes have on their grades. Try asking your students what their average would be if they began the year with two one hundreds and then forgot to turn in a project that also counted one hundred points. Most will say "C" while some will say "D." A few others might even guess "B," and one student with a calculator will tell you the truth. The average will be a 67. In many schools, that is a failing grade. The students that guessed C or B are truly in danger of having zeroes destroy their grades.

In order to explain the power of zeroes, ask your students to visualize a number line that runs from the classroom door to the opposite wall. Stand next to the door and take several sideways steps toward the opposite wall. Explain to them that the space between you and the door represents the passing range. Then show them the difference between you and the opposite wall far away in the distance. That is the failing range. Ask the students to pretend that a zero were in the middle of the line where fifty resides on that number line. If a zero were at fifty, the failing range would still be three times larger than the range for any other grade. The problem with a zero, though, is that the zero is fifty points lower than that!

The solution we suggest to the problem of zeroes is an acronym we picked up at a High Schools That Work Conference many years ago. That acronym is ZAP, or Zeroes Aren't Permitted. Before explaining what ZAP is, it is necessary to explain what it is not. ZAP does not mean that a teacher does not assign zeroes. We have worked with schools that have done away with zeroes and made the lowest possible grade something in the neighborhood of a sixty. We firmly believe that this is a mistake. It might make sense for assignments that have been honestly attempted; however, a fifty or sixty for doing nothing sends the wrong message. The way to get students to succeed is not take away the chance of failure. True success is overcoming failure. True success is learning from failure and then doing better the next time. In fact, we contend that if there is no possibility of failure, then there is no possibility of success. If a student never turns in an assignment, then a zero is the appropriate grade.

Instead, ZAP is a philosophy that must be shared by both students and teachers. A learning skill that freshmen must possess if they are to be successful is to understand the negative impact of zeroes and to not allow themselves to ever get a zero. Successful students will always turn in something. Even if they end up with a fifty on the assignment, turning it in is better than getting a zero. Too often, though, students do not give the teacher an opportunity to award a fifty. Instead, for whatever reason, they fail to turn in work. Students must be taught ZAP.

ZAP must also be a philosophy of teachers. The teacher's responsibility is twofold. On the one hand, teachers must teach students about ZAP. Teachers must work to help their students understand the importance of turning in work. At the same time, teachers must be willing to give students second chances to overcome the bad academic decisions they make. If not, then the teacher will not have an opportunity to give a fifty to the freshman who did not turn in something on time because he or she is still learning to believe in ZAP. This might mean that the team of teachers should accept late work. More on this topic will be discussed in chapter 10.

JOHN WOODEN'S PYRAMID OF SUCCESS

For freshmen to be successful, it is imperative that they understand what success is and how it is attained. Many students have the wrong idea or a limited idea of success. Success is more than money and fame. It is more than being a professional athlete or a movie star. Success is living an autonomous life. Success is being free to live the life you choose, to be able to support yourself and those you love, and to be able to take advantage of the many opportunities that are available in our country.

John Wooden, the legendary UCLA basketball coach, is an amazing teacher of success. He says that success is "the peace of mind which is a direct result of self-satisfaction in knowing you did your best to become the best you are capable of becoming." To illustrate this he created his Pyramid of Success. The Pyramid gives students a structure that they can follow to change their lives and achieve a personally satisfying success.

Wooden's Pyramid is comprised of what he has identified as the fifteen building blocks of success. Each block is placed in a specific place for a specific purpose. At the top of the Pyramid lies Competitive Greatness. The beauty of Wooden's Pyramid is that it gives students a visual of what they should be doing in their lives. Everyone can relate to Competitive Greatness. Whether on the playing field, in the classroom, on the job, or in one's relationships, Competitive Greatness in life is what all people are striving to attain. By taking time to teach students about the Pyramid, students can learn to set goals for themselves and then learn step by step how to attain those.

For more information on John Wooden's Pyramid of Success, we recommend that readers visit www.coachwooden.com or read John Wooden's book, *They Call Me Coach* (1988).

Some readers may be wondering just how all these learning skills can be taught. Who has time to teach about Choice not Chance, S.L.A.N.T., Victim Statements, the Role of Failure, ZAP, and the Pyramid of Success when there are so many state standards to meet and end-of-course tests for which students must be prepared? This is once again an area in which teaming reveals its power. Four teachers working together can effectively teach these ideas. For one teacher to try to do it all would be difficult. The power of four, though, allows teachers to do more than they ever thought possible.

If the root causes of low achievement lie in students' attitudes and learning skills, then these areas must be addressed in order for freshmen to be most effectively transitioned into the high school.

Chapter 6

Organization and Time Management

Have you ever noticed that your freshmen have trouble with organization and time management? The lack of organizational skills is a great impediment to the success of our students, especially for our freshmen. As educators we can complain about our students' poor organizational skills all we want. We can bemoan the fact that they lose things, that they do not know how to take notes, and that they forget to do their assignments. This complaining and bemoaning rarely leads to change, though.

On the other hand, we can take a more productive tack and do what educators do best—teach. We can actually teach our students how to be organized. We can teach our students how to take notes and how to plan. We can hold them accountable for the behaviors that will lead to success while demonstrating for them how to exhibit those behaviors. We can provide them opportunities to practice organization and require them to take advantage of those opportunities.

Teaching beats complaining every time. When it comes to teaching ninth graders organizational skills, the first step is to tackle the problem as a team. As we have discussed many times previously, trying to single-handedly change the culture of a student body is a difficult task. A team that is in the life of a student for at least half of the student's day has a much greater ability to mold and shape. As a team, decide what organizational behaviors your students most need. Then teach them.

Students need repetition, and they need to be held accountable. So the next thing you need to do after identifying the behaviors your team will teach is to decide how students will be held accountable for the behaviors. Probably you will choose to involve grading or points of some sort. In behavioral modification terms, as educators we do not give students cheese to get through the maze; we give them points. The connection between being organized and having academic success is important. One of the best ways to help our students understand that the relationship exists is to make sure it is a reality in our classrooms. While we do not want to create an atmosphere of grade inflation in which a student can achieve high grades simply by being organized, the importance of organization is easily worth a slight increase to a grade.

STRATEGIES FOR ORGANIZATION AND TIME MANAGEMENT

We doubt very strongly that there are limits to the number of methods and strategies that a team of teachers could use to reinforce these behaviors in students. Once again, then, what follows is by no means an exhaustive list of ideas. In fact, we have chosen to focus on only two areas of organization and time management. You and your team will probably choose others beyond these; however, we have found that the following two strategies are easy for a team to teach and are a tremendous help for students.

UNIFIED NOTE-TAKING SYSTEM

The first organizational strategy we would suggest is a unified system of note-taking. While at times it is fashionable to speak of note-taking as an outdated practice, we contend that taking notes is a time-tested and proven strategy that when used properly is often the most efficient means of conveying information for later use. Research has repeatedly shown the benefit of writing down information for later study. Note-taking is an important skill for students to learn, as it will serve them well in high school, in post–high school education, and in life.

There are several problems with note-taking, though. First of all, many students do not know how to take notes. Secondly, many, if not most, of our students do not know what to do with their notes once they have been taken. An effective team of teachers can fix these problems.

If all the team teachers use and require the same note-taking system, reinforce that requirement, and teach students how to use notes for studying, then students will have a better chance of becoming effective note-takers.

More than likely you will need to periodically check notes. For example, each teacher might check a random set of notes once or twice a week. If the students have the notes, they should receive partial credit, but if the notes are in the proper format, then the student might receive full credit plus an extra point or two. While this grade should not be too large in the scheme of a grading period, it can serve as a strong motivator for doing things the "right" way.

It probably does not matter what system you use; however, we would like to suggest a specific system called Cornell Note-Taking. This system was developed by Cornell University and is the best way we have seen to teach students to take notes that are organized and that are easy for later studying. Here's a suggestion: Google the phrase "Cornell Note-Taking". You will find numerous sites that describe how to set up notes in Cornell.

In the Cornell system, students draw a line from the top to the bottom of their page of notes before any notes are taken. This line is called the Cornell Line. The Cornell Line should be about one-third of the way across the page from the left-hand margin. (see Figure 6a) Any notes should be taken on the right-hand side of the Cornell Line. Then, after the notes have been completed, the students should create, on the left-hand side of the Cornell Line, questions that correspond to the information found on the right-hand side. These questions are called Cornell Questions.

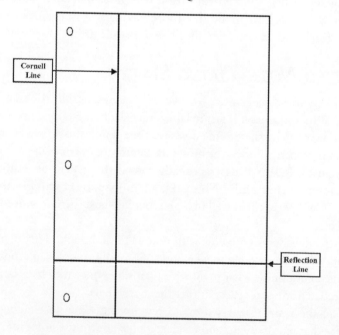

Figure 6a. Cornell Note-Taking is simple to set up.

For example, if the notes were about Winston Churchill, the questions on the left might be asking where he was from or what he did that was important. Creating these questions can be a homework assignment that will cause students to review their notes. It can also be an in-class assignment. This method provides the teacher with an opportunity to go over the notes with the students to check for their level of understanding.

After students have created their Cornell Questions, they should draw a line across the page from left to right at the end of their notes. Below this line is where students will create a reflection. The reflection is their attempt at higher-level thinking. For example, after reading back over their notes once again, they might compare and contrast the notes with another topic, form an opinion about the topic covered, or make a prediction on what will happen next.

Students will often have difficulty creating a higher-level reflection. Common reflections early in the year might include, "These notes are nice," or "I like this topic." Team teachers must take time to reinforce the idea of higher-level thinking. Perhaps you might choose to give your students a question to answer for their reflection that will require them to think deeper than they otherwise would. Here, though, is another place in which the power of four becomes a factor. Four team teachers reinforcing this system will have a powerful impact on a group of students' ability to become higher-level thinkers.

Just think about what Cornell note-taking has caused to happen. First of all, your students have taken their notes while listening to you discuss them. Next, they have had to look back over the facts in their notes in order to create their Cornell Questions. In order to write their reflection, they have had to think about the topic as a whole. Finally, when it comes time to study for a test or quiz, the students can cover up the notes and ask themselves the Cornell Questions. If they have done a good job writing their questions, they have probably just asked themselves the entire quiz or test.

Sometimes, because Cornell Questions and the reflection require more paper than ordinary note-taking, students will try to say that they do not want to use Cornell. The same students that do not mind littering are suddenly environmentally friendly and concerned about the unnecessary use of paper. The reality, though, is that Cornell notes are a good use of paper because they help students learn.

Cornell is easy to learn and can be applied to all subject areas. English teachers can use it in reverse as a guided reading activity. Simply give the students the Cornell Questions and have them fill in the notes as they read. Math teachers can have students solve problems on the right-hand side of the Cornell Line and then write the appropriate property, theorem, or formula on the left. Science teachers can use Cornell to help students with labs. The reflection is essentially the lab conclusion. History teachers will appreciate the way Cornell Questions help students learn facts.

Cornell causes students to analyze the notes they are taking, stimulates higher-level thinking, and provides an incredibly useful study tool. Most importantly, though, it is a strategy that, when reinforced by a team, will enable ninth graders that have trouble with organization to become effective, organized note-takers.

STUDENT PLANNERS/AGENDA BOOKS

The second organizational strategy we find vital to the success of ninth graders is the use of a student planner or agenda book. Student planners can serve as either your number one organizational tool or as your number one waste of money. They are not cheap. Therefore, if your school is going to take advantage of this incredible resource, it must do so properly.

Simply having a student planner is not enough. A school must first design its planner with success in mind. Then it must ensure that the teachers who will be using it (we recommend starting with your freshman team teachers) are trained on how best to do so. Finally, it is imperative that the students are trained to use the agendas and required to do so.

Most agenda companies provide certain stock pages to which you will want to add your own. Your day timer pages will be some of the stock pages. These pages provide a place for your students to write down their homework. We suggest that part of each class's daily Do Now assignment be to write down the homework for that night in the student agenda. Remember, because your teams have made the Do Now assignment a standard expectation, this will be much easier to accomplish than it would have been if you were trying to do so on your own.

Students will only do this if you require them to do so. But if they do, what a great communication tool you have just created. As we mentioned earlier, we advocate homework every night. Parents have already been told, "Don't ask your child if she had any homework. She has homework every night." Now you can also tell parents to ask their children to let them see the agenda. The parent not only knows there is homework but can actually find out what it is.

It is important to have a plan for requiring the use of agenda books. The first step is to make it a team practice and part of the expected culture. Next, you need to grade it. Once a grading period, each teacher on the team can check his own section of the agenda. For this purpose it works best if you purchase an agenda that has each day in a column with rows across the days for each subject. That way the teacher can quickly scan a week. If homework is written for each night, then the student gets the full grade.

The next thing that needs to be in your student planners is a Record of Achievement or a place to record grades. Your agenda company probably will not provide enough space for this, so we suggest adding several pages of grids. Require your students to write down each grade they receive. This way they can easily calculate their grades at any time. Again, you will probably need to grade this to reinforce the habit. Once a grading period, maybe while the students are taking a test, collect the agendas and make sure the students have enough grades written in them.

Useful agenda books also need to have the student code of conduct, school tone schedules, and who in the school students should see for various needs they might have. These should be included as part of the pages your school inserts at the beginning of the agenda book. Think about how much money is spent in most school systems printing nice-looking codes of conduct that just end up in the trash. By diverting that money to your agenda books, you will defray some of the cost. Plus you will be putting the code of conduct in a place that will be accessible at any moment for students, parents, and teachers. These items will also make the agenda a more relied-upon tool. For example, students rarely remember their school's early dismissal schedule. Now each student will carry it around with them everyday.

Consider using the cover of your agenda for several purposes. Most companies allow you to design your own custom cover. On the back, try putting a copy of your school year calendar. Be sure to include on this not only the standard dates but also when your freshmen progress reports come out and when report cards are sent home. Use your front cover to express the ideals for which your school stands. For example, you might have messages regarding success, achievement, and recognizing students. You might collect names each spring of students who have achieved at a high level and then put these names on your cover so your students can begin to see that your school recognizes hard work and success.

We have run into many individuals who tell us that they do not need to be convinced of the effective possibilities of agenda books. The problem they see, though, is getting students to bring them to class. The answer to that problem is easier than you might think. First of all, do not order the typical high-school size agenda book. Most companies have a small high-school size. Instead order the 8.5 x 11 book that is usually referred to as a middle-school size. Your students will not know the difference unless you tell them. The benefit to this size is that it will fit perfectly into the notebook you require all your team students to use.

However, the main way to guarantee that your students will bring their agenda books everyday is to make the agenda book the uniform school hall pass. If students know that the only chance they have of getting out of a class is to have an agenda book, then they definitely will bring their agendas.

Perhaps the organization and time management problems facing your students were not addressed in this chapter. Even so, the method for doing so was! The method consists of a team of teachers identifying the problem and then developing a means of consistently addressing the problem. There is no guarantee that you will solve all the problems of organization and time management that your students have. However, a team of teachers that works together to teach and reinforce skills can go a long way toward helping students gain the ability to organize and plan for success.

Chapter 7

Parent/Teacher Contact

One of the most important factors affecting student success is appropriate parental involvement. Therefore, it only makes sense that educators interested in improving student performance should be interested also in improving contact between the school and the home.

Some parents understand the importance of communicating with the schools and take it upon themselves to make sure communication occurs. However, many students have parents with very negative views toward education. In many cases they have been hurt by their own schooling experience. Their view of communication with the school is that no news is good news.

Perhaps some seemingly non-communicative parents do not mind communication but instead lack the knowledge of how to be properly involved with the high school. The elementary years were easy. The student had only one teacher; therefore, the parent had one point of contact with the school per year. At the high school level the child has at least four teachers and as many as seven or eight depending on the type of schedule used by the school. To make matters worse, because high school students have the negative distinction of being teenagers, they are actively discouraging their parents from even attempting to figure out how to communicate with all these people. Furthermore, many parents have the false belief that now that their child has made it to high school, it is time for the parents to be less involved. These factors, coupled with busy lives, make it very difficult for many parents to have the appropriate involvement we all know to be so important.

If a team of teachers is going to effectively impact student behavior and attitudes, then it must have a plan to harness the power of parents. Or, if circumstances necessitate, the team must find ways to help weaker parents stay on top of their children's progress. Teachers must make parents aware of life at school, both the positives and the negatives. Schools must sell their ideas, their programs, and their beliefs to the parents and the community at large so that they can help them understand that the system is there for them.

Throughout this book we have discussed the power of four. Four teachers working in conjunction simply have more power than four working individually. More positive and more productive contact with parents is yet another potential benefit of the power of four. Your team needs to take advantage of this power as you deal with parents.

Parent/Teacher Contact Strategies

Here are some ways in which the power of four can increase parent/teacher contact.

Team Planning

Team planning time, as previously discussed, is a tremendous resource for meeting with parents. With today's large number of single-parent families or families with two working adults, it is very difficult for parents to come in to meet with teachers. However, as part of a team, you will be able to avail yourself to parents any day of the week. What a great blessing for parents to be told that they can pick any day they want at a certain time and be able to meet with as many as four of their child's teachers at a time. Too often parents feel as though they are forced to drastically alter their schedules to meet the needs of the school. The convenience of team planning helps perpetuate the idea that the school is there to meet the needs of the entire family.

Team Web Site

Chapter 8 will discuss in greater detail the benefits of having a team Web site. For now, it will suffice to say that a team Web site where, at the very least, all homework is posted plays a major role in the effort to enhance parent-teacher contact.

TEAM E-MAILS

For better or worse, e-mail has changed the way the world communicates. Use it to your team's advantage. At the beginning of the school year, collect e-mail addresses from your students and from their parents and then create an e-mail list. You might need to send a note home requesting these addresses. Throughout the year, as you meet new parents, be sure to update this list. Each week send out a team e-mail letting parents know what is going on at school. Include upcoming assignments, winners of your incentive drawings, ideas and advice for helping students succeed, and anything else that your community would appreciate. The feedback you will receive will be overwhelmingly positive.

ENCOURAGE PARENTS TO E-MAIL TEACHERS

Another way to use e-mail is to encourage parents to e-mail the team teachers. Recently we spoke with a high school administrator. We were encouraging her to enhance the use of e-mail communication. Her reply was shocking. She stated, "I don't give out my e-mail address to anyone other than teachers in our school system." What a waste of an amazing communication tool! Think about the occasional phone calls from parents that you receive or did receive in the days before the heavy use of e-mail. While you may be thankful to have an opportunity to speak to a parent about a student, phone calls tend to interrupt time that teachers spend with their families. However, what is worse than the interruptions is the fact that the phone allows for such a limited amount of communication. Typically only a small handful of parents will call a teacher during a school year. With e-mail, though, it is not uncommon for a teacher to receive over one-hundred and fifty e-mails from parents in a school year. Those e-mails never interrupt dinner. Teachers can respond to them at their convenience, even during team planning time, to include input from all four teachers. Most importantly, those e-mails help parents help their children. There is quite a difference between one-hundred and fifty e-mails and a handful of phone calls. Increase your productive parent contact by encouraging people to use your e-mail address.

TEAM STANDARDIZED EXPECTATIONS

Consistent team policies also enable better parent-teacher contact. In the same way that standardized procedures help students understand what is expected of them, fewer sets of rules and expectations help parents know how to guide their children. For example, once a parent knows that homework is assigned every night, the parent has an easier time staying on top of things.

When the parent further knows that the homework should be written in the agenda book for each class, then the parent is easily able to determine whether or not his child is doing what is expected. When you take away the perception of "it's too much to keep up with," your parents will be better suited to do what it takes to encourage their child's success.

FRESHMAN ORIENTATION

Set up a Freshman Orientation night and go over these expectations with parents. Explain team practices and procedures. Help them understand your goal of transitioning their child into high school. Discuss the role that parents play in this process. Describe team planning, the team Web site, and how to use e-mail to communicate. Explain agenda books, homework policies, the Do Now, and team notebooks. Go over all the things that the parents need to know for their child to have success.

When setting up this orientation night, do not be influenced by the naysayers who predict low attendance. It is true that high school events are usually not as well attended as such meetings were in elementary school. Therefore, your job is to give people a reason to attend. Sell the meeting well. Run the meeting well. Use it as an opportunity to tell parents how much you will love their children and to show them all that you do to help them be successful. If you do, over time word will get out in the community that this is a meeting parents do not want to miss.

We can complain about students' poor choices. Or we can teach them how to choose. We can bemoan the fact the students are irresponsible. Or we can teach them how to be responsible. Likewise, we can complain that parents are not properly involved. Or we can use the power of four, the power of a team, to help parents become involved.

Chapter 8

Technology

Better uses of technology are yet another potentially positive outcome of working as a team. Before giving some examples of ways your team can grow technologically and use technology to better transition your freshmen, it is worth reflecting for just a moment on the role of technology in education.

Technology for technology's sake is a waste of time. But if technology can be used to enhance learning, to draw students into the educational process, and to better transition freshmen, then how can a teacher not be willing to try it? Once upon a time the blackboard was new technology. There were probably some "old dogs" at the time who were lamenting the loss of hammers and chisels, or whatever was used prior to the blackboard. However, the blackboard worked better. Likewise, when other new technologies come along that work better than what has been employed, teachers are foolish not to try them.

There are a couple of negative reactions that often result when the word "technology" is used in educational circles. Some educators agree that a new technology might work better, but they do not feel as though they have time to learn the new trick. Enter once again the power of teaming. A team that meets everyday can use their team planning as a time for learning "new tricks." Set aside time regularly to share strategies with one another. If one of you is great with PowerPoint or Inspiration Software, teach the others. If one of your group's members can make Web pages, learn from that person. Your transition program has a built-in time to learn.

The other negative reaction to technology stems from the fact that not all schools have made the same level of investment in it. Many teachers would love to try new ideas, but their schools currently do not provide the necessary resources. That is unfortunate, but we would encourage teachers to consider a couple of additional realities. Your school is headed in the direction of new technologies. Even the most backward of schools are much more advanced today than they were ten years ago. The trend in all schools is in the direction of more technology. Secondly, the power of four can help your school. A team of teachers has a louder and more potent voice than an individual. One teacher requesting new technologies can easily be overlooked, but a team of teachers making such a request in order to transition freshmen into high school has a much greater chance of being heard.

There are several technologies that can be used to help Freshmen Transition Programs attack some of the problems faced by freshmen. For example, many freshmen do not believe that the system, the school, is there for them. Therefore they spend time fighting the system. Another problem many freshmen share is that they lack the type of attitude regarding education that leads to success. Technology, specifically digital photography and PowerPoint, can help with these problems.

As a team, take photographs of your students in class, around school, at practice, at various activities, and around town. Then make PowerPoint slide shows of your students set to music. Your students will love the fact that you take their pictures. This simple act serves as a wonderful example of how much you care. When the students see the PowerPoints, they truly appreciate the effort. They love seeing themselves. It is almost as if they were on television.

For your slideshow music, choose a song that has a message or moral. After the class has had the fun of watching the show, take a few minutes to explain to them why you chose the song. Through this relatively simple activity, you have shown your students that what they do interests you and that you are willing to take extra time to make something fun just for them. By doing this, you have earned the right to be heard. In other words, your brief "sermon" on why you chose the song is being heard by ears that care what you know. This is because, as the saying goes, they now know that you care.

Another issue that often plagues freshmen is that many lack an understanding of what goes into earning good grades. Many have difficulty taking ownership of their grades and the decisions that led to them. Technology can help with this problem as well.

Many high schools provide electronic grade books to their teachers. More than likely in these schools teachers are required to submit their grades via these grade books at the end of every grading period. This is an example of how technology can make our lives easier, but the power of an electronic grade book is even greater than this. Teachers need to truly use their electronic grade books. The key word in that statement is "use." Rather than keep grades in a conventional grade book and then transfer them to the electronic one at the end of the grading period, the team teachers should keep all grades in the electronic grade book as they are graded. By doing this, the teachers truly harness the power of this technology.

Often freshmen have trouble understanding the impact that their work, or lack thereof, has on their grades. They view grades as something teachers assign rather than something that students earn. The use of the electronic grade book can change this. When grades are kept in the electronic grade book, students and parents can receive feedback at anytime. Progress reports can be printed out and sent home, or can be turned into PDF files and e-mailed to parents. Students can see immediately the impact of the most recent test, quiz, or assignment.

Earlier we discussed that students do not understand the power of zeros. The next time a student fails to turn in an assignment, pull her up to your desk. Show her the impact that the missing assignment is having on her average. Then show her what would happen if she had turned in the assignment. Show her what even a 50 percent grade would have done. More than likely the student will ask, "Can I still turn it in?" You might answer, "Sure, but only for a 50 percent." Something powerful has just happened, though. The student who did not care about the zero is now asking to do work. *Using* an electronic grade book is a powerful use of technology.

In the previous chapter, we discussed the importance of increasing communication between school and home. Here is yet another place where new technologies can work better than the old ways. In today's information age, the Internet has taken communication to a whole new level. Your team needs a Web site. What many teachers do not realize is that making a Web site is as easy as typing a letter with Microsoft Word. If you can do that, you can make a Web site. Plus, a team-planning period gives team members a time and place to learn. A team Web site should be, as best as possible, a "one-stop shop" for team information. Be sure to include links to your e-mail addresses, and be sure to include your daily homework assignments. These two items alone will do wonders for communication.

Technology can allow the following scenario to become a reality. Because you have homework every night, your students' parents no longer have to ask if there is any homework. Instead, you have taught your parents to ask to see the agenda book. However, some of your students have decided that they can escape having to do work if they just tell their parents that they forgot to write down their homework in the agenda. So now parents can check homework online. If a student is trying to avoid the agenda, a mother can now check the homework hotline and ask the child directly, "Did you do the activity for chapter 3, section 2?" For just a moment the student is convinced his mom is all-knowing, but then the student thinks of a new way out. He tells his mother, "I left it at school." The student is impressed with his mother's detective work, but smiles in knowing that he has one-upped her. However, the mother replies, "I'm glad to help you out, dear. I printed out a copy of the activity while I was at work." The mother hands the print-out to her son and thinks to herself that she sure is glad your team has a Web site.

That scenario is easy to make happen. Once your team has a Web site with homework listed and your e-mail addresses, you can begin determining what else can go on the site. A goal to consider is to have all your work, notes, and assignments archived and downloadable. While to some readers this may sound like a lot of work, remember that you have a team-planning period to work on it.

A team Web site allows students who are absent to keep up with their work. It enables parents to better hold their children accountable. Homebound instructors can teach students with their own notes and assignments from the Web site, and students who move to your school during the school year can use it to catch up on what they missed.

There definitely exist old ways of doing things that should continue, but there also exist many newer methods that are more effective. Your team should be on a mission. You are striving to meet the needs of your ninth graders as never before. Use your time in team planning to explore, practice, teach, and learn. Find new methods that work better, and then put them into practice. Your students will benefit, which is the purpose of all instructional tools, both old and new alike.

Chapter 9

Student Recognition

Human beings have a fundamental need to be recognized. Whether for who they are, what they have accomplished, or how they have lived, within all people there exists a desire to be recognized. Some seem to desire this more than others; in fact, some seem to go out of their way to gain the attention of others. But even among the quiet and introverted, the desire to be recognized in a positive way remains strong.

Teachers are well aware that the drive to be recognized runs strong within students. In some ways, it seems to be the very essence of being a high school student. Pursuing athletic endeavors, wearing outlandish clothing styles, joining clubs, striving for the honor roll, cutting up in class, being negative, forming cliques, not caring about anything, and performing in the band all serve as examples of high school students seeking to fulfill this very basic need.

Have you ever noticed that there seems to be a connection between academic success and the recognition one seeks and receives? Students who feel as though they play a vital role in their school community succeed at a higher rate than those who feel ostracized. Recognition leads to students believing that they belong and that they have a place within their school.

In fact, studies have shown that the most common reasons for dropping out of high school are attitudes toward school, relationships with teachers, poor school performance, and a sense of alienation from the larger school environment (Lan & Lanthier, 2003). Positive recognition can have an impact on several of those factors.

Educators, though, are well aware that not all recognition leads to positive results. When it comes to academic success, there is positive recognition and negative recognition. Our job as educators is to provide students with opportunities for positive recognition that will fulfill their natural desires and lead to academic success.

One reason some students end up turning to negative forms of recognition is that they believe themselves incapable of receiving recognition for anything positive. Typically they think themselves not smart enough, not good looking enough, or not athletic enough. For whatever reason, they believe that brains, looks, and talent are the only ways to receive positive recognition. Once they become convinced that the pursuit of these traits is an impossible endeavor, they tend to do one of two things. Either they begin pursuing negative means of receiving recognition, or they give up altogether and decide they will never be a part of the school community.

Neither of these two alternatives can be acceptable to educators. If our students are going to make the most of their high school experience, they must feel as though they belong, and they must receive positive recognition at school. Nowhere is this more critical than during the freshman year.

There are countless indicators within most schools that freshmen do not belong to the same degree that upperclassmen do. The students in the school who are the most insecure and the most desirous of attention are the ones who have the most difficulty finding positive ways to receive attention. Typically, there are fewer opportunities for a ninth grader to contribute to the school community. This is one of the major reasons why so many of our young people get lost during that transition year. If they cannot make a name for themselves through sports, if they are not attractive enough to stand out from the crowd, if they are not at the top of the class academically, how else will they contribute? In their minds, they are "just freshmen." Unfortunately, this negative self-concept often leads to them seeking attention in ways that are self-destructive and that run contrary to what they should be doing to succeed in high school.

Teachers of freshmen must set goals to provide these students in transition with positive recognition. They must look for opportunities to create a sense of belongingness for them. Students need convincing that there is a role for them in their school and that their basic need for attention can be met in a positive and productive manner.

This is no small task. In some cases, teachers of freshmen will be attempting to undo as many as fifteen years of conditioning. Prior negative schooling experiences will have to be battled. Teachers will be acting as a counterweight to negative messages from the home about education, perhaps even struggling to overcome generational ideologies and weaknesses.

Freshman teams have a unique opportunity to affect the culture of schools. The smaller learning community created by the teaming structure affords teachers the opportunity to impact students in more than just their own classroom. By working together through standardized procedures and practices, teams can create an environment in which students feel recognized, rewarded, and appreciated. Four teachers working together have the ability to make school a truly cool place.

There is no magic formula for student recognition. There is no one correct way to do it. As long your means of student recognition encourage students to act productively, reward them for behaving positively, and create a sense of belonging, then you are moving in the right direction.

It is also important that the recognition be real. In other words, students need to be recognized for something they have actually done. The goal is to create a mental and physical connection between doing what is right and being successful. The goal is to create a positive self-concept. The goal is not to create students who are happy and full of self-esteem. Empty praise and self-esteem building lead to unrealistic expectations in young people. External praise that is not based on actions devalues praise. Our students need to be given opportunities to act productively and positively. Then they need the praise. This reinforces the idea that they can control their success. Their self-concept ultimately needs to be a result of their own internally motivated decisions rather than extrinsic rewards. Extrinsic rewards are not bad, but they must be tied to actions.

RECOGNITIONS STRATEGIES

What follows are some ideas for student recognition that we have tried, liked, and seen used well in many schools. This list is by no means revolutionary; however, when these methods and strategies are employed by an entire team, they can go a long way toward convincing students that their school is a place in which they can receive positive attention and recognition.

BRAVOS

We first learned about Bravos at an AVID conference. (AVID stands for Advancement Via Individual Determination and is an organization we would recommend highly to all educators.) Bravos are a simple way to elicit positive classroom actions from your students. Get several sticky note pads and a rubber stamp that will not be easy to duplicate. Stamp the sticky notes and keep them in your desk. These are your Bravos. When a student exhibits positive classroom behaviors, such as great answers or thought-provoking questions, give that student a Bravo. Just stick it on the student's shoulder or desk and say, "Bravo!" You will get major results from this minor act of recognition. Earning Bravos can be a goal of review games or even quizzes. They might become redeemable for points or for homework assignments. However you structure it, you will be pleased with how much your students will want to earn Bravos.

STUDENTS OF THE WEEK

To many high school teachers, the practice of naming a student as the Student of the Week might seem rather childish. It is amazing, though, how much freshmen enjoy this. Each week, each teacher on the team picks a student of the week. The student can be selected for any reason the teacher desires. Maybe they have been doing a great job all year, or perhaps they might have finally shown improvement. Whatever the reason, the student receives the recognition they crave. Try putting certificates on your wall to publicly recognize the students of the week. Be sure to tell your class why the student received the honor. You might give the student of the week a copy of the certificate to take home. Many parents of high school students have reported to teachers that they have posted these certificates on refrigerators or have even taken them to Kinko's to have them enlarged into posters.

CLASSROOM HALLS OF FAME

At the end of each grading period, each teacher on the team can find a creative way to recognize students who have achieved at a certain level. Students could be recognized for earning A's, for improving at least one letter grade, or for having averages above ninety or above one hundred. Perhaps you might have multiple levels of recognition. Whatever your criteria, make it a big deal. Post it in your class, and put the list on your Web page. Send the names to your parents in an e-mail or newsletter. Announce it to everyone and encourage all students to make the list next time. Try to find a creative and appealing name for your list. Perhaps your A students could be the Knights and Ladies, with the highest averages being the Dukes and Duchesses. Call your top achievers the History Hotshots, the Top 7 Wonders of the World, or the Stellar Excellers. Whatever the title, your room will become a place where achievement is recognized and encouraged. Freshmen truly appreciate this.

INCENTIVE DRAWINGS

At the beginning of the year, have a big fundraiser or, if your school system allows it, solicit donations and prizes from local businesses. This may seem like a big job, but since you are on a team, you are not the only one working on it. With multiple teachers taking part, the odds are great that you will either raise a lot of money or an abundance of prizes.

Throughout the rest of the year, give away the money and prizes to your students. There are many ways to do this. One method that has been used successfully at many schools is to have regular "name in the hat" drawings. Whether at the end of every week or every grading period, or before special dates, give your students a chance to put their name in the hat for their accomplishments. You choose what these accomplishments will be. Some ideas are perfect attendance, earning an A or a B, not being suspended or getting detention, being the student of the week, and having all homework completed. Then periodically draw names and give away prizes. The size of the prizes will be determined by the amount of money raised or the number of prizes collected.

So start thinking. What can your team of teachers do to recognize students? It is the job of educators to create the climate that rewards positive behaviors. If schools do not give students positive ways to earn recognition, they will find their own ways to be recognized.

Personal Voices

In my own school we have held drawings at the end of each grading period. Each team will typically give away around $300 at each of these drawings. The top prize is $200, and then various other prize denominations make up the remaining $100. We have held special drawings for grades earned in the weeks leading up to Christmas and Spring Break. You should see what this does to the level of academic effort during a time when students typically slack off. At the end of each year, both of our teams has a special assembly. At this assembly many awards are given out—most helpful student, most improved English student, best female Algebra student, etc.—but the most fun part is giving away the really big prizes. Each of our school's teams typically gives away $1,000 to an individual student at these assemblies! Some people might say we're paying students to do a good job. I would agree. What's wrong with that? I don't hear adults complaining about being paid to do their jobs. One teacher once complained that our incentive drawings were extravagant. I told that teacher he was correct. They are wonderfully extravagant! And most importantly, these drawings recognize student achievement, reward positive behaviors, tell students they belong, and make school cool!

—Scott Habeeb

Chapter 10

Support Services

MULTIPLE POINTS OF ENTRY

No matter how phenomenal your team program is, and no matter how talented your teachers are, there will be some students who are not successful. You will get some kids onboard with your incentives, while your standardized expectations will help another set of students succeed. Four team teachers using the same classroom leadership techniques will help ensure positive results for others. But there will exist still that small population of students who seems destined to not complete the ninth grade.

The *Wall Street Journal* is a modern version of the vertical layout scheme that was used in the earliest newspapers. If you want to get into the story, if you want to learn the information, you start at the top of the first column and read on. *USA Today*, on the other hand, uses a modular layout. If you want to learn what it has to offer, you can read the text, study the graph, or read the summary. It is possible that the *Wall Street Journal* has better information in it, but few would argue that it does as good a job as *USA Today* in relaying that information to the typical reader. The *Wall Street Journal* is the highbrow paper of the educated. *USA Today* is the paper of the masses.

Think of teachers as newspapers. We are charged with relaying information to a certain population. We have a duty to make sure our "readership" hears "the news." If we are vertical layout newspapers, or *Wall Street Journals*, then

60

our readers must be reading at the beginning if they are going to get the news. This is not always the case, though. In classroom terms, what happens when some of our students are not onboard at the beginning of the year? Will their lack of preparedness, maturity, and diligence at the beginning prevent them from ever entering the story?

Teachers of freshmen need to be like the *USA Today*. They must provide multiple points of entry into the story of education. If students decide one-third of the way through the year that they are ready to work, will it make a difference? If students finally realize that they are capable of reading the story, will it be too late because the vertical layout only had one beginning? Or can teachers, like *USA Today*, create charts, graphs, summaries, tables, and pictures that allow students to begin the reading of the story that will better enable them to live their lives to their fullest potential?

Too often in education, students have no way to redeem themselves from poor choices. It is possible to have a student score so poorly during the first few grading periods that success will elude them no matter how great an improvement they make the rest of the year. Students like this quickly deteriorate into behavioral problems, and tend to have a negative impact on the entire classroom.

Are classrooms like trains that leave that the station at the beginning of the year, making no stops to pick up passengers until they start the journey again the following year (or semester on a block schedule)? If so, then we must realize that we will leave behind any youngsters not ready to board.

The phrase "No Child Left Behind" has been taken over by politicians, and as a result has become rather controversial. And yet as educators, the idea of No Child Left Behind must be our purpose. Our profession is about giving all students the tools necessary for success. We are educating the masses, not the few. The real teaching glory comes when the hardest to reach are reached. Many other students will learn in spite of us. We must not forget about those who will only learn because of us. They need us the most. Teachers who wish to taste of this glory must have plans in place to allow students onboard the train even though the journey has already begun. To open the doors of opportunity to all students, teachers must be like *USA Today*, and provide multiple points of entry into the story.

It is our view that in order to adequately provide multiple points of entry into the content of our classrooms, especially for freshmen who are young, yet who must make choices with long-lasting effects, teachers must have support systems in place that afford students with second-chance opportunities to recover from poor academic decisions.

MULTIPLE POINTS OF ENTRY PUT INTO PRACTICE

There are many ways that schools might provide multiple points of entry for students. The methods chosen by schools will be determined by resources available, the type of master schedule used, personnel issues, and student needs. For example, some schools have tutorial sessions built into the master schedule. Others might have after-school transportation available. One school might take advantage of the fact that several teachers like arriving to school an hour early. Another might have a grant that allows it to hire additional staff. Each of these factors, and many more, will impact the specifics of a school's support services plan. We have chosen to share a few ideas that your school might want to take into consideration. As you read them, contemplate how they could be adapted to meet your school's individual needs.

LATE WORK

Freshman Transition Teams should give great consideration to establishing late policies that change as the students mature. Many teachers are inherently predisposed against the idea of allowing late work. Teachers are interested in holding students accountable and in teaching students the importance of deadlines. We agree wholeheartedly with these sentiments.

At the same time, we also question which of the following is more important—*when* a student does work or *that* the student does work. In our opinion, if the assignments are meaningful and lead to learning, then whether or not a student does the work is a bigger issue than when the student does the work. We cannot focus on doing work on time until we get students to do the work in the first place.

Another idea is to consider is the age of the students with which we are dealing. Freshmen are young. They are incapable of always making the right decision. However, the decisions they are making have the potential to impact the rest of their lives. This does not mean that they should not have to make good decisions or be held accountable for their actions. What it does mean is that teachers need to keep the complete picture in focus. Many universities will allow students to carry an incomplete for a period of time. Even graduate schools allow grown adults this privilege. Some high school teachers, though, have a problem allowing a ninth grader who has barely reached puberty a single extra day to undo the negative effects of an immature decision.

In most cases, late work should probably have a penalty associated with it. Perhaps it will be for a lower grade, or maybe the late assignment will be longer than the original. Students could be required to do the work in a detention or on a Saturday. These are all issues that the Transition Team can work out together. What is important, though, is that the students who did not do their work the first time are given an opportunity to do it, and by doing so, gain access back into the curriculum and have a chance to learn.

Keep in mind that many students agree with the teachers who are opposed to such second chances. These students do not want to do the work. They would truly appreciate being told that late work is not accepted. This would provide the perfect excuse: my teacher would not let me do the work.

What follows is an example of a way that a Transition Team might collaborate on a late policy:

For the first semester of a course, or perhaps first grading period if on a block system, the team can choose to be quite liberal in its late policies. Each teacher might have to be a little different depending on the nature of the work that is late. For example, it would be more difficult for an English teacher to receive twenty late papers on the last day of a grading period than it would be for a history teacher to receive twenty late sets of definitions. So while each teacher might have slightly different standards, all teachers on the team would choose to be forgiving and allow late work to be turned in throughout the grading period. The work will probably have a grade penalty, but it will be accepted.

After the semester, or after the early grading period if on a block, the liberal late policies would begin to tighten up. Students would be allowed to only turn in work up to a week past the deadline. That work would only be worth 50 percent, whether it was turned in one week late or one day late. After one week, it would not be accepted. Finally, during the last grading period of the year, or the last grading period of the semester if on a block, no late work would be allowed at all.

Several important things have occurred as a result of such a policy. For starters, at the beginning of the year, the students were *not* allowed the option of *not* doing work. Secondly, by being made to do the work, they learned that work is important. Then, as doing the work increased their grades, they began to better realize the relationship between doing work and earning strong marks. Finally, by the end of the year, the student has learned how to turn work in on time, a major goal for transitioning freshmen.

AMNESTY DAYS

Amnesty Days refers to the idea of offering students an opportunity to fix poor academic decisions. Amnesty Days are different from simply turning in late work; they are typically one-shot deals that are sold to the students as big events. For example, a team might allow students to come in on one particular Saturday and make up or redo any work from the grading period. Perhaps the last week of the grading period could have before-school Amnesty Days. Monday morning could be a chance to redo English, Tuesday could be Science, and so on.

As with the late work policy, the amount of credit should probably lessen during the year in order to transition freshmen out of needing such opportunities. Perhaps the first grading period's Amnesty Day could result in making up work for 100 percent credit and bringing your average up two letter grades. The next grading period might be only worth 80 percent. Later in the year, students might only be allowed to bring an average up by one letter grade, and at the end of they year, there might not be an Amnesty Day.

As a team, sell such an opportunity to your students when the opportunity arrives. (We recommend not telling students about such opportunities on day one of the school year.) Work together to help students understand that you are concerned about their education and that you are giving them a chance to get back in the game. Once they do the work and begin raising their grades, preach to them about how much easier it would be to do this work when it was due the first time.

CREDIT RECOVERY PROGRAMS

A Credit Recovery Program is the final means we will discuss for providing multiple points of entry. Credit Recovery is an opportunity for a student who earns an F on a report card to raise the grade to the lowest possible passing grade.

Picture for a moment the student who after a grading period or two is completely out of the game as far as passing the class you teach. What happens to that student? More than likely, he or she becomes either an overt discipline problem or a classroom sleeper that detracts from the successful culture you are trying to create. Credit Recovery serves to provide that student with an opportunity to undo the failing grade, get back into the curriculum, and then move successfully into the future.

There are many ways to structure Credit Recovery. One way is to hold it after school with each day focusing on a different subject. If a freshman fails English for a grading period, then he could stay after school on the day that English Credit Recovery is offered, probably for an hour or two. The student would first notify his English teacher of his intention to stay. The English teacher would then leave individualized assignments with the Credit Recovery tutor/teacher. The student would work on the assignments after school and receive help and assistance from the tutor. The completed work would be collected by the tutor and given the next day to the English teacher. The English teacher would review the work and determine whether or not the student had done enough and done it well enough to earn the passing grade.

In this model, the number of days that the student would need to stay per subject area would be determined by the classroom teacher. The teacher would base his or her decision on how much work the student did in Credit Recovery, how low their failing grade was to begin with, and what types of assignments the student needed to do to bring up their failing grade. Some students would take the entire next grading period to fix the failing grade of the previous, while some would only need a week or two.

In order to make sure that students do not simply stop working during the day in order to make everything up in Credit Recovery, it is important to stipulate that in order to raise the failing grade to passing, the student must successfully and adequately complete the assignments left by the classroom teacher AND have their current grading period grade at the passing level. In other words, if a student successfully re-took tests and quizzes from the first grading period but still had an F average for the second, then the student would need to continue attending Credit Recovery until he or she was also passing the current grading period.

When students attend Credit Recovery for a grading period, successfully complete prior assignments, but do not bring their current grades up to passing, it would make sense to at least raise the student's previous F to a higher failing grade. To not do so would make a student feel as though he or she had worked for nothing. However, to reward increased learning with an increased average is completely reasonable and teaches the right lesson, even if the new average is still an F.

Whether your Freshman Transition Program uses a unified late policy, Amnesty Days, a Credit Recovery plan or some combination of the three, you must find ways to keep struggling freshmen in the ballgame if you are going to transition them into high school. While it would be wrong to take away the option of making bad decisions, it is right to provide students with opportunities to recover from the ones they make.

Do not forget that in each of these support service models, the students are working. While to some it might seem as though life is being made too easy on the students, the reality is that it would be easier for them to not have to work. By working hard and finding success, even if it occurs in an alternative setting, your freshmen will learn the skills they need to be successful and will appreciate the school that gave them the opportunity.

Personal Voices

I have heard some argue that giving second chances makes school too easy. They may even say that teachers in favor of second chances are lowering the bar. These people need to be told the story of Shamu.

If you have ever been to Sea World, you have certainly seen the amazing tricks that Shamu the killer whale performs. However, killer whales do not instinctively want to jump high into the air to perform for spectators. They have to be trained. Many of our students do not instinctively want to do the work we ask of them. They, too, must be trained.

Ken Blanchard's 2002 book, *Whale Done!: The Power of Positive Relationships*, discusses the way Sea World trainers use positive reinforcement to train Shamu. In order to teach Shamu to jump on command, a bar is placed under the water. When Shamu swims over it, she receives positive reinforcement. The bar is gradually raised and each time Shamu goes over it, positive reinforcement is received. The bar is eventually raised out of the water, and finally no bar is even needed. Shamu has learned that jumping up earns positive reinforcement.

Shamu would never have learned this lesson if the bar had not been lowered at the outset. Perhaps giving second chances to a freshman is lowering the bar, but if in the end the student performs better than ever thought possible, who could argue against it?

—Scott Habeeb

Chapter 11

Organizing Your Teams: All the Same But Very Different

This chapter is intended for educators who think that all this sounds good, but who really need to know how it can work in *their* school and for *their* students. It is also designed for the administrators and counselors who will be creating the infrastructure that will allow the Freshman Transition Program to exist.

Unlike many challenges facing public education today, problems with freshmen, including poor attendance, high incidences of misconduct, and low academic achievement, are prevalent in urban, suburban, and rural schools. Students both with and without disabilities, from poor and affluent neighborhoods, and of all ethnicities impact their futures with the choices they make during their ninth-grade year. The problem with freshmen transcends geographical, socio-cultural, ethnic, and economic circumstances. That is the bad news. The good news is that the freshman opportunity transcends the same factors. In other words, solving the freshman problem will lead to school transformation regardless of the school's socio-economic status.

Our experience working with schools representing a very wide range of demographics has led us to conclude that while there is no universal solution, there is a nearly universal process. Each school and each community will have a different set of resources and tools available. Therefore, there is no one-size-fits-all solution. What has been described in this book is a process. The key components of a Freshman Transition Program, first outlined in the diagram at the end of chapter 1, and then discussed throughout this book, will look very different depending on the school in which it is implemented. However, any school can address the issues outlined in that diagram, and, if done successfully, transform itself from the bottom up.

When creating your Freshman Transition Program, it is imperative that this concept is kept in mind. Your goal is not to do exactly as a neighboring school has done. Instead, your goal is to address the key components in your school's own unique way.

Another key idea to keep in mind during your planning phase is that the most important place in any school, including yours, is the classroom. That is where the interaction between teacher and students exists and where the transaction of teaching and learning occurs. No matter where the school and no matter the demographics of the community it serves, if a problem is to be changed into an opportunity, it is in the classroom, under the leadership of the teacher, where the change will occur. Therefore, administrators and those responsible for creating the school's Freshman Transition Program must seek to do so in a manner that will enhance teacher effectiveness and empower teachers to maximize their potential. The key decisions made during the creation process will determine the impact of your program. That puts a large burden upon administrators and planners. On the other hand, what can be more exciting for an educational leader than knowing that your decisions have the potential for long-lasting, school-changing effects?

WHAT ABOUT THE MASTER SCHEDULE?

Administrators and educational leaders reading this book have more than likely been asking themselves questions such as "Which classes should be teamed?", "Which teachers should be part of the program?", "Which rooms should be used?", and "How can this fit in the master schedule?" These are key questions that have to be answered if a program is to have success. Like so many elements of our schools, it all starts with the master schedule.

First, it is important to understand some basic master schedule concepts. A school's schedule affects every student and every teacher several times every day. This is why a good schedule is so important. If, however, your schedule, or your conceptualization of a schedule, is preventing you from doing what works and what most helps freshmen be successful, then the schedule itself needs to change.

We are not advocating for one type of schedule. A Freshman Transition Program, like all smaller learning communities, can function within a traditional or block (4 x 4, semester, alternate day, or flexible/modular) schedule. Our experiential bias favors a traditional schedule because we think that the chances for helping freshmen transition are increased when the team teachers see the student four or more times a day, five days a week, for an entire year. Furthermore, a student's chances of being changed are better when he or she is in the care of four different but similarly committed teachers preaching the same message. However, we have helped schools with all types of master schedules implement successful transition programs. What is most important is for educational leaders to set as a priority the creation of a schedule that will best allow the school to implement each of the components of a successful program. While we do not advocate one particular type of schedule, we do advocate making sure you have the schedule your school needs, even if that means a major master schedule change.

WHICH STUDENTS?

Team Design Pitfall # 1
Starting small with only "at-risk" students

Many educators ask the question "Which students do we want to schedule onto our teams?" This question is understandable; however, it is the wrong question to ask and ends up making scheduling more difficult before the process even starts. Instead of choosing students, choose courses. By selecting courses that freshmen typically request, you simplify the staffing decisions that you will need to make, and you avoid the potentially slippery slope of picking students.

While one of the main reasons schools consider transition programs is to help struggling students, we have found that the most successful programs target as many students as possible. In cases where planners are directed to start small, the temptation is to start with only the most at-risk students. However, this is a common mistake.

Although starting small with the most at-risk freshmen is appealing to administrators seeking to make the most of limited resources by allocating them to the students who need them, this is a common pitfall that can inadvertently stigmatize the students involved and even the entire program. Even if the year goes well and the data indicates that the first year was successful, a program that focuses on the most difficult students runs the risk of burning out the teachers who boldly began the program and may encounter resistance from students and parents the following year who are reluctant to participate in a program that was for "bad" or "dumb" kids the year before.

Furthermore, teaming only at-risk students prevents heterogeneous grouping. Weaker students need to have opportunities to work with stronger students. Less-motivated students need an opportunity to see what hard work looks like and to be in an atmosphere conducive to success. In homogenous grouping, the weakest, least-motivated students, often with the most behavioral problems, have only each other for role models. These students end up spending every moment with one another. As the school day progresses and they move from room to room, the negative factors seem to increase.

By choosing which courses to team-teach instead of the students, you have the added benefit of randomly assigning students to teams. If you cannot team all or most students, and often this is the case in the first or pilot year of a transition program, random assignment of students will provide a heterogeneous group and a representative sample that will serve you well when you compare the group's progress to the non-teamed students.

Random assignment of students is a generally good approach to building a transition program, but there are limits. An appropriately used "scouting report" from your feeder middle school(s) will enable you to separate students who are more likely to succeed and less likely to interfere in the teaching and learning process if they are not in class together or even on the same team. Further, an administrator can use the information in a completely professional and appropriate manner to inform a team of teachers to work closely with students who may need extra help in their academics and/or their decision-making.

WHICH ROOMS?

Some Freshman Transition planners opt to use classrooms in close proximity. Some have even created separate schools for freshmen. Typically the term "Freshman Academy" is used to describe these situations. Our experiences support the effectiveness of both of these and none of these. First, isolating freshmen in a separate building or school certainly creates a smaller learning community, and the results in terms of student learning, attendance, and discipline are generally very impressive. School districts choosing this option, however, need to plan for the tenth-grade transition. The grade level is not as significant as one may think. A large number of our nation's high schools are configured to serve grades 9–12 and in these schools, ninth graders distinguish themselves for the wrong reasons. If you were to pay a visit to a school with a less common configuration, such as a senior high with grades 10–12, or a junior high with grades 7–9, you would likely see the same problems in the tenth grade or seventh grades, respectively. The fundamental truth is that people of all ages struggle with change.

How you configure your rooms is not overly important. Our suggestion is to find what works best for your school's physical plant and your school's culture. Does your school prefer to be organized by departments? Then keep it that way. Your freshmen will benefit from having to learn how to traverse the crowded hallways in a short period of time. Traveling across a crowded building is what high school students have to do, and your goal is to transition these students into high school.

Does your school have a wonderful wing that is just waiting to be better utilized? Then use it for your freshmen. Make it a place of positive attitudes where a culture of success is emphasized in each class and on every wall, and where teachers can work together to encourage each other to find new ways to meet the needs of freshmen.

What is most important regarding room selection and location is that the configuration decision is based on what will work best for the freshmen and the teachers in the program. The goal of the transition program is not to hide freshmen from the rest of the school. Be wary of individuals who may sound as though they want to support the program, but in reality are trying to remove the freshmen problem from their presence.

There is one more idea to consider when deciding which rooms to utilize for your transition program. We recommend giving team teachers, even if they have less seniority, their own rooms so that the students in the program always know where to find their teacher. There is a slight benefit for the master scheduler here. Because team planning is generally held in the team leader's room, schedulers can assign other classes into the rooms used by other team members during the team-planning period. This has the added benefit of "encouraging" those teachers to move on to team planning in a timely manner because another teacher and class are arriving.

WHICH TEACHERS?

When selecting teachers, the obvious question that must be answered is who the best teachers for a transition program are. Obviously you need teachers of different content areas. We generally recommend that you use teachers from the four core areas. This is not because other subjects are unimportant, but because we want to target as many students as possible, and most all students are taking classes in the four core areas. We are often asked if there would not be a great benefit from including the band director, PE teacher/coach, or career and technical teacher on a team since these teachers are often skilled at creating personal connections with students. The answer is that it would be great to have every teacher of freshmen on the team, but in reality the students need to be in class somewhere when the team of teachers is meeting for its common team planning.

We are not suggesting that non-core area teachers are not tremendous assets. If fact, we like to refer to them as "encore teachers." When we help schools establish transition programs, we find that one of the most successful approaches includes a presentation to the entire faculty. This process encourages the faculty, including the encore teachers, to see itself as having a role in this most important of missions. If these teachers will support the transition program, for example by sharing some of the standardized expectations or by finding ways to recognize students, then the program's overall effectiveness will increase significantly.

An important and potentially sensitive aspect of assigning teachers to teams involves personalities, experiences, and relative strengths of teachers who will be serving on the teams. When assigning teachers to teams, it is generally advisable to consider the following for compatibility and a good mix of skill sets:

- Personalities of members
- Strengths of members
- Ability to achieve consensus

In terms of personalities, you obviously need people who can get along on a team, yet you would not want all of your assertive classroom managers on one team and all of your newer, technologically savvy teachers on the other. You need a good mix of experience and skill on both teams, but most of all, you need people who can agree that, first and foremost, they are there to meet student needs and not their own. Teachers concerned about student success are willing to compromise when collaborating with a teacher who does things differently.

Team Design Pitfall # 2

Assuming that all great teachers will make great team members

---

There are extremely effective teachers who are not cut out for team teaching. Clearly there are ways to assist, support, and guide teachers to grow, but this is not a book about developmental supervision. In our experience, when faced with an effective teacher who works magic in the classroom but who demonstrates an inability to compromise, it may be a wise decision to look for another teacher who can work well on a team. This teacher will likely become a more skilled teacher in the process and allow the King or Queen their own kingdom in which to work their magic.

Team Design Pitfall # 3

Assuming that the teachers on a team should remain the same each year

---

Staff changes inevitably occur. When multiple vacancies on one team of teachers occur at one time, serious consideration should be given to reassigning a member of an intact team with good dynamics and proven results. We can tell you from experience that the team that is asked to peel off a person or two will likely resist and will make good arguments against the separation. They will pledge to support the new team if only left intact. However, the experience and talent levels of teams need to be balanced while cultivating talent for the future. Moving a member from an especially strong team to bolster a team in transition simultaneously creates an opening for a new hire to serve on an already proven team. With guidance and supervision by the administration to ensure that the new teacher's gifts and points of view are welcomed, the team-planning period will provide an ongoing and meaningful opportunity for mentorship.

WHICH COURSES?

Student requests should drive the master schedule process. This includes decisions regarding which courses will be team taught. Start by considering which courses most of your students request. In most cases it is easy to identify which English, science, and history/social science course most freshmen take. The challenge usually involves mathematics because students generally track into different math courses beginning early in middle school. Because math courses frequently represent the most homogenous groups of students, it is absolutely essential that a balanced number of sections of the different math courses offered are assigned to each team. This ensures that you do not end up with a "smart team" and a "dumb team."

To illustrate this point, consider a school with two teams using a traditional seven-period day, where teachers teach five classes. In your case, the numbers of students, courses, and teams may be different, but the point here is that special consideration should be given to having a good mix of students on the teams. Using district guidelines regarding class size, student requests result in the number of sections illustrated in Figure 11.1:

Course	Number of Sections Needed
Algebra 1 Part A	4
Algebra 1 Part B	4
Geometry	2

Figure 11.1. Sections needed

The wrong way to team these courses would be to place an emphasis on reducing the number of preparations that teachers have. Such an emphasis might result in a configuration of math courses similar to the one illustrated in Figure 11.2.

Course	Team X	Team Y
Algebra 1 Part A	0	4
Algebra 1 Part B	4	0
Geometry	1	1

Figure 11.2. The wrong way

In this case, each math teacher has only two preparations, but Team X will likely have more academically inclined students than Team Y because every student on Team X took and passed a high-school math class at the middle-school level. As a result, the English, science, and history/social science teachers on Team Y also will have a different level of student than their counterparts on Team X.

In an effort to make the teams more heterogeneous, consider the configuration in Figure 11.3.

Course	Team X	Team Y
Algebra 1 Part A	2	2
Algebra 1 Part B	2	2
Geometry	1	1

Figure 11.3. The better way

In this case, Team X and Team Y are much more likely to be heterogeneous, but the math teachers will have three preparations. In reality there are multiple ways to go about assigning and staffing these sections. The main point is that including a mix of math courses across your teams is a tool for creating heterogeneous grouping in other teamed classes.

Now Schedule It

Newer scheduling algorithms accommodate teams, but even the most antiquated student information system can schedule teams by creatively using Student Requests, Course Numbers, and Class Capacities. Even if you are required to use the same course number for all English 9 classes, you are not printing transcripts the summer before students enter the high school, so temporarily using different course numbers can help separate students into teams. For example, assign students with course number English 9 – 1145 on one team, and students with course number English 9 – 9145 on the other.

Another trick is to set the maximum class size on all sections that are not on a team to the minimum, which is usually one (1) student. Then schedule the students from one team. After one student is scheduled in the wrong sections, the algorithm identifies those sections as "full" and only schedules students into the desired sections, which are the ones with regular class capacities. Next, manually remove the one student from the other sections into the desired classes and then set those sections to a class size of one (1). Because the previously scheduled sections now appear "full" to the scheduling algorithm, the next group or team of students are scheduled into the open sections and so on, as many times as needed, depending on how many teams you will need to serve the students.

These are only a few of the techniques that can be used to have the desired outcome. We share these strategies to make the point that if the individuals responsible for the master schedule really want to schedule teams, they can. However, doing so requires making it a priority.

Be warned that there are sacrifices. Scheduling an unencumbered Team Planning period may involve giving some senior staff members duties that they have not had in while. In Block Schedules (both 4 x 4) and Alternate Day, it will likely be necessary to divide the 90 +/- minute planning block. This represents a significant change for team teachers in some schools. In our experience, it is absolutely essential to schedule Team Planning during the first-half of the block. It is tempting to make a case for giving teachers the first half of the block to take care of their individual planning needs, but in most cases, the individual time gradually increases. As team members arrive just a little bit later each week, team-planning time is eroded.

Team Design Pitfall #4

The Pack of Wolves: giving groups of similar students similar (or identical) schedules

---

Easier is not always better, and that is definitely true when scheduling students for a transition program. The easiest way to schedule is to give a group of students the same schedule, so that when twenty-five students finish English, they all move as a group to science at the same time that the science group is moving to Algebra. This is a recipe for disaster. As the school year progresses, the students become more and more tired of each other and less and less patient with one another. Furthermore, this scheduling model will cause weak students to never gain the benefit of seeing more dedicated academic role models. Certain classes of English will be enjoyable for the teacher and others will be nightmares. Observing a class change in the hallway under this model is like watching packs of angry wolves moving from den to den.

PROVE IT WORKS!

As with any new initiative you undertake, it is imperative to institute systems of mutual accountability and annual evaluation. A first and simple step is to maintain a Team Log. A Team Log will almost certainly contain anecdotal information, but a purely narrative log will be of limited help when it is time to report the results of the new initiative. Starting each year with tally sheets for conferences with students and parents, as well as counselor and administrator visits, permits the teams to report out at anytime during the year how their time is being used. Thirty to forty parental contacts a semester above and beyond the school's regularly scheduled conference days is not unusual and is a powerful measure of increased parental involvement.

The administrator responsible for overseeing the Freshman Transition Program should visit every team every week. He or she should vary the arrival time, ask that the visit be recorded, and periodically ask for a total number of visits by the administrator and the counseling staff. This helps ensure frequent communication and simultaneously conveys an unspoken message that team teachers need to be on time and on task for the team-planning period.

Plan to have the team teachers meet for at least one day every summer to evaluate the previous year and make plans for the next. By having the teams meet together, even in a social setting, early in the summer, a comprehensive report can be quickly prepared. The program administrators should specify what information will be requested at the beginning of the year and provide tables or other templates so that the teachers involved know exactly what information is needed and in what format. Near the end of the first year, and every three to five years afterward, a presentation should be made to the school board to ensure that the governing body is informed so that they can remain supportive.

HOLDING TEAM MEMBERS ACCOUNTABLE

Time is money. As professional educators, we must always seek to be good stewards of resources. When planning to implement a transition program that is built around a team-planning period, it is helpful to communicate the investment that team planning represents. One method is to compare the fraction of the school day that will be devoted to team planning with the same fraction of a new teacher's salary. Figure 11.4 shows an example for a program on a seven-period day that will have two teams of four teachers:

Beginning Teacher Salary	$30,000
Beginning Teacher Salary/7 periods	$4,286 per period
Salary per period x 8 teachers	**$34,286 – school's investment in team planning**

Figure 11.4. A school's monetary investment in team-planning periods

For the $34,000 shown in Figure 11.4, the school system could offer more study halls, have more teachers on hall duty, patrol the parking lot better, provide assistance to the attendance office, or offer special tutorials to students in need of assistance. The provision of a team-planning period is truly an investment. Team teachers must respect that investment by using the team-planning period effectively. If your program is designed properly from the start with high expectations created and agreed upon by all for all, then this should not become a problem. However, it is imperative to keep in mind the necessity of using this resource wisely.

EMPOWERING TEACHERS

Team teachers will be working harder, teaching more effectively, and helping more students experience success. To help them accomplish this, we feel that administrators must empower teachers to do more and, in the process, change the way that students view the teachers and even how the teachers view themselves.

One of the many added benefits for a team of teachers sharing a group of students is the ease with which they can change a student's schedule. Team teachers are able to identify situations in which a student may be removed from one class with negative peer dynamics and placed into another class. Therefore, team teachers need to be given the power to change the order of a student's day. Parental permission is not necessary because the student's teachers do not change as long as the change is always intra-team. It is only necessary to involve an administrator or a counselor so that the schedule change can be reflected in the student information management system.

Because a team of teachers working together has an inherent system of checks and balances, they can be trusted to have the power to assign disciplinary consequences beyond the norm for a teacher in your school. We have observed great success in schools that allow team teachers to assign a few disciplinary consequences that have typically been available only for administrators.

For example, many schools have a Saturday Detention. In schools that offer Saturday Detention as an alternative to Out of School Suspension, provisions and procedures can be established for teams to assign students. If the team of four teachers unanimously agrees that a student would benefit from Saturday Detention for misconduct, or because he needs to complete some missing assignments, they need only meet with the student, call his parent, and e-mail the administrator who sends the regular school letter regarding the detention. In our experience, teams tend to use this power sparingly. Typically, the contact with parents are positive since parents understand that this decision is not just one person's idea and is intended to help their child.

Team teachers can also be involved in the scheduling of new students. Often, when a new student enrolls in a school during a school year, a school counselor develops a schedule for that student that is based almost exclusively on class size. The problem is that the smallest class may not be the best place for a new student. New students need opportunities to feel welcomed and begin to be a part of the life of the school. With team teaching in place, the school counselor need only visit the next team-planning period and ask the team teachers in which class periods they would like to have a new student. The first consideration from teachers tends not to be to place the student in the smallest class. Rather, teachers tend to undergo a much more thoughtful process of which class has a group of students, a lab group, or even just one peer leader who could best help a new student get onboard.

In practice, this approach operates as follows: The new student arrives one morning, and the counselor identifies on which team the student will likely be placed. The counselor asks one student from that team to be a peer guide for the new student on the first day while the paperwork and schedule is worked out. The counselor visits the team-planning period to determine when the new student's core classes will be. Toward the end of the day, the counselor lets the new student pick from available electives and provides a copy of the schedule for the following day. Note that thanks to teaming, a day is not lost with the new student simply shadowing some random peer. Although the new student's schedule will likely be different, it will include most of the same teachers.

The provision of resources, the participation in program development, and other forms of empowerment like those listed above have both a direct and an indirect impact on how teachers are viewed. Successful team administrators will value their teachers as leaders within the learning community. This results in the students' perception of teachers being rapidly altered. When they discover that team teachers can change their schedule and even assign consequences that used to require a trip to the principal's office, they gain a new respect for these teachers. The teachers' self-perceptions change when they experience the additional authority and responsibility that is afforded them.

A Freshman Transition Program, as we describe it, is not a one-size-fits-all idea. How you team is going to vary from school to school, and, in some cases, from year to year. However, by following the guidelines and principles detailed here, an innovative and imaginative administrator can make teaming a positive reality for his or her school. The result will be a school that is transformed from the bottom up.

Chapter 12

You Gotta Believe

In the world of public education, programs and ideas come and go. Fads start and fads end. However, great ideas need to last. If great ideas benefit young people, then educators cannot allow those ideas to fall by the wayside.

Your school's Freshman Transition Program should contain your own version of the elements described in chapters 2 through 10. Administrators should pay careful attention to the pitfalls and suggestions outlined in chapter 11. However, if change is the ultimate goal, then the roots of the freshman problem must be addressed. To not address the root problem is like putting a Band-Aid on a broken arm.

In this chapter, author Ray Moore will write in the first person as he addresses the root of the freshman problem—the problem of believing. It is the contention of this book's authors that the content of this chapter is what will make or break your transition program. In a sense, the best and most important has been saved for last. Excellent plans and systematic approaches will be partially effective at best without the words that Ray Moore is about to share. Once the framework outlined in the previous chapters has been created, then the team teachers must take advantage of the opportunities afforded them and work together to focus on what is most important: becoming more effective teachers who understand the deep needs of freshmen and work together to meet those needs.

The Dream

One morning in early August of 1994, I walked out of my house and closed the door on the first phase of my career. I did not know it then, but I was preparing to take a journey across country that would give focus to my calling.

My assistant principal at the time had asked several teachers to go to an AVID (Advancement Via Individual Determination) conference in San Diego. The most important thing that I learned at this conference came unexpectedly in a speech that I thought would be boring. As has often been the case in my continuing education, one thought buried in a book or in a class can change the way I think about my students and about education. One of those ideas was waiting for me in the keynote speech of that conference. This idea gave focus to my vision of education. The superintendent of San Diego schools said in an address to the conference participants, "It is the responsibility of schools to give everyone access to the American Dream. First, we must make students believe they can have access to the dream. Then we must give them the tools to achieve it."

I am not sure that I had ever heard anyone say that schools had a responsibility to address attitudes. I had often heard that schools had to give students the tools to achieve success, but this superintendent was saying that *first* we had to address the issue of students believing certain things. Those words shouted out to me, and echo louder and louder into each day I spend in the classroom.

These words are even more important today as schools focus on high stakes end-of-course testing. We are inclined to focus so much on filling kids' heads with the facts that we feel as though we have little time to address more fundamental issues of attitudes and of believing in something. This is the wrong way of looking at our time. If we truly want to be successful with our students, in particular with our freshmen, our best use of our limited time is to focus on these ideas above all others.

Believing

Parker Palmer, in *The Courage to Teach* (1997), says that American high schools have become an assembly line of classes where we "wheel" students into a room and try to infuse them with facts like patients hooked up to an intravenous feeding tube. When the period is over, we "wheel" them to the next classroom and repeat the process in another subject. Palmer notes that we complain that they seem to be apathetic, but he points out that they are not apathetic in the hallways.

The truth is that students are very excited and very interested in some things. Quite often those things are not the things we would like, but every teacher knows that students, especially ninth graders, do have energy, and they do not lack ideas.

Quite a few students actually are interested in the subject matter, or they are interested in doing well. Many students possess the kind of belief systems that will help them succeed in school. On the other hand, there are a large number of students who have no belief system or who have seriously flawed belief systems.

Part of the reason for this is that today's society is far different from the one that existed seventy years ago and more. People were not perfect in the days of the Lone Ranger and Mickey Rooney films, but society agreed on what the model of perfection looked like. Today, those models are diminished. In some ways that is good, but in other ways, it is not. Systems such as the church and the family have a less significant role in society today. Many people have little understanding of concepts like humility, service, and giving. They do not understand that it is important to believe in something. They do not understand the role that believing plays in shaping our character and in giving strength to our character. Instead, they believe that strength is found in how loud they can yell and how successful they can be in finding flaws in others and in destroying the creation of others.

In the movie *Second Hand Lions* (Kirschner, 2003), Robert Duvall's character is talking to his nephew one night. The nephew is demanding to know if the heroic stories he has heard about his uncle serving in the French Foreign Legion are true. The uncle tells the boy that it does not matter if they are true, but the boy protests. His mother lies to him all the time, and the truth does matter to him. The uncle, however, insists that it does not matter if the stories are true. He tells his nephew, "If you want to believe in something, then believe in it! Just because something isn't true, that's no reason you can't believe in it! … A man should believe in those things, because those are the things worth believing in."

What we believe in defines who we are. Therefore, as teachers interested in helping ninth graders define themselves and begin successful high school careers, we must spend time addressing believing. Remember, part of transitioning freshmen into the high school is preparing them to be successful beyond the freshman year. Imagine what it would be like if each student who came through our program left with a strong and positive belief system intact. This is what we mean by transforming a school from the bottom up.

I believe in my children. That does not mean that I believe that everything they do is noble. It means that I will risk everything I have and everything I own on them because they are worth the investment to me. That is the kind of belief system that many of our freshmen lack. They do not believe that there is anything worth believing in that does not have a clear and immediate result.

Because of insufficient value systems, freshmen are vulnerable to the false values with which they are inundated each day. They will do anything to be accepted. Schools often do not see this situation as a problem that is in their realm to address. However, that view ignores the obvious impact that these insufficient value systems have on a student's academic success—the stated realm of every school system.

Our ninth graders do not need a soft belief system that promises everything they want if "they will just believe." Our students need to understand and value the kind of faith that can transform their lives and help them rise above themselves. That kind of belief system is one that will not only help them believe that they can have access to the American Dream, but it will also help them stand against the stupidity hurled at them that says it is cool to be dumb, or it is cool not to do the work that will help them succeed. This kind of belief system is based on a faith that is bigger than an individual and whether that individual will get what he or she wants. Martin Luther King, Jr. changed the face of America with a nonviolent movement that some in society would never have believed could have worked. Students need such heroes whose belief systems changed who those heroes were and then changed the world in which they lived.

Students need belief systems that will change who they are and carry them into the future. Our students need an alternative to believe in that will give them an opportunity to leave behind the mistakes they have made in the past and leave behind the false images they have about strength. Too many weak students think posturing and showing others how tough they are is what strength is.

Students need a belief system that will sustain them through disappointment and dark days. They will need to learn to work and wait as Ray Kinsella says in the novel *Shoeless Joe* (1999). Ray heard the famous voice say, "If you build it, he will come." Ray did build the baseball field, but Shoeless Joe did not come. He did not come for three years. Ray must have questioned himself over and over. He must have wondered if he had ever even heard the voice. He must have questioned if all the work and risk of his farm was worth it. He complained that it was not fair. He said, "I have to work—and wait."

That is exactly what many freshmen lack. I have met many students who lack the ability to work and then keep working when Shoeless Joe does not show up immediately. Some kids have parents who teach them this skill, but many do not. Many of the best athletes in our town never played high school ball. Sometimes, it was because they got in trouble. Sometimes, it was because of grades, but often it was because they quit sports before they ever got to high school. They got on bad teams and got tired of losing, and they had no one who could help them understand that there are times when a person has to work—and wait. They had no one telling them what it was that they did well or who would tell them to focus on what they could do well instead of what they could not do.

LESSONS FROM MY CHILDREN

When my son Seth was a junior in high school, he was a leading quarterback in our section of the state. The local newspaper wrote an article about him and the pressure involved in being the quarterback of a program in a "football town." Seth said in the article that he decided he wanted to be the quarterback in that town when he was in the fourth grade. He said that there were many people who told him he would never be the quarterback because he was too small, because his arm was not strong enough, and because there were other players who were better than he was. He had to suffer through losing seasons and times when he was passed over for the all-star teams. Even some coaches told him that he would never make it.

Seth, however, had a poem on his wall that said, "When the struggle seems all uphill, that is when you must not quit. Many a failure is one who never learned that success was just around the next corner."

Obviously, Seth did become the quarterback when he reached high school. In fact, he earned first-team all-state honors, but he would not have done so if he had quit because of the discouragement of others and the negative circumstances he faced. As a matter of fact, Seth was recruited to play at a prep school after high school. Most of the players there were true Division I players who needed to improve their grades. When we got there, Seth was intimidated by the players he saw. There were kids who could run a 4.2 forty, and there were players who weighed 300 pounds and were pure muscle. When I was turning to leave, Seth said, "Hey, Dad, do you think I belong here?" I said, "I guess we will find out." A week later, Seth was the captain of the team.

Seth had a difficult time in prep school because of the competing demands of the military side and the football side. He was under constant stress, and he was away from home for the first time. I would call him often, and he would always complain about his conditions. One night I asked him if he wanted to quit. He became incensed. He said, "I have never quit at anything, and I am not about to start now!" Seth finished the season and was offered a full football scholarship to attend college. Interestingly enough, he turned down the scholarship and decided it was time to get serious about preparing for a career. Seth is now a senior financial analyst for the world's largest defense contractor and has earned an MBA. Our freshmen need examples like Seth, and there are many such examples to share to teach them about never quitting.

At the beginning of each school year, I tell my ninth graders that someone once asked Socrates, "What is the best way to get to Mt. Olympus?" The answer Socrates gave was, "By making sure every step you take is in that direction." After a discussion of what Mt. Olympus is to us today, and how close our steps have to stay to the path, I tell my students a story about my daughter Moriah.

Moriah started her educational career by having to repeat the first grade because of a reading problem. In the fourth grade, she decided that she wanted to attend Duke University. She had no idea how difficult that road would be, but she believed that she could take certain steps that would allow her to achieve her dream. She began an eight-year journey to gain acceptance to Duke. She began playing sports in middle school hoping that athletics might help her get in. As she was entering the ninth grade, she made a bold move to switch schools, so she could pursue the prestigious International Baccalaureate Diploma that was not offered at her school. The new school also offered a more competitive athletic program. Moriah was unsure if she could even make the team at her new school, but she knew that as Ray Bradbury says, "Sometimes you have to jump off cliffs and build your wings on the way down."

As it turned out, Moriah did make the teams. In fact, she was the first freshman to ever start on the varsity volleyball team at her new school. She ended up as the captain of each team she played on during her junior and senior years. Academically, Moriah had to work very hard. She regularly pulled "all-nighters" through her time in the International Baccalaureate program. She studied on the bus on the way to games and in the stands when the junior varsity was playing. After four years of hard work in high school, Moriah, the girl who had to repeat the first grade because of a reading problem, was one of ten students in her high school to earn the International Baccalaureate Diploma.

In the fall of her senior year, she applied for early decision to Duke and was deferred to regular decision. At regular decision, she was told that Duke thought they might be able to offer her admission in August, but Moriah decided she could not wait. Instead, she accepted admission to the University of Virginia and entered as the equivalent of a second semester sophomore with fifty-three college credits that she earned in high school.

The lesson in Moriah's story is powerful. She believed in a dream that did not come true. She never made it to Duke. Some people might view the story as proof that believing is pointless, but I tell my students something else. I tell them that Moriah's story illustrates that I cannot promise them that they will reach their Mt. Olympus—even if they take every step in that direction. However, I can promise them that the journey will change who they are.

Moriah began her educational career as a failure, having to repeat the first grade. She ended that career as one of the top students in her school, and it was not just her grades and her achievement that changed. The quality of her thinking and her living grew as she sacrificed to reach her Mt. Olympus. When she graduated from the University of Virginia, she joined the Peace Corps to give service with humility to people who were born into circumstances less fortunate than her own. Our students need this kind of belief system to give them the faith that they can have access to the American Dream.

THREE THINGS TEACHERS MUST BELIEVE

Before schools and teachers can begin to build these belief systems in students, the teachers need to do a belief check on themselves. There are at least three things that teachers must believe if they are going to be able to get freshmen to reach these new heights. After all, when it comes to the classroom, it all starts with the teacher.

The first and most important thing that a teacher must believe is that the subject matter is important. Many might feel as though that statement goes without saying, but there is more to it than may be apparent. Parker Palmer in *The Courage to Teach* (1997) says that teachers begin their careers full of good intentions and good will. He says that teachers share who they are, and they share the subject they love. They make themselves vulnerable to their students, and they are answered with spit balls and shouts of "Can we do nuthin' today?" and "This class is boring!"

After days, weeks, and years of this treatment, without even thinking about it, teachers take a step back and begin to build a wall. They involuntarily become less vulnerable and begin to cover material rather than inspire students. It is not that the teacher does not think that the subject matter is important; it is that the teacher does not think the subject matter is important to the students. Palmer describes good teaching as "an act of hospitality toward the young" where the teacher shares the subject they love with the student. At their best, teachers who share their love of the subject with the students will infect the students with enthusiasm for the subject.

That is not possible when a teacher has taken a step back and begun to just go through the motions. The "courage to teach" is the courage that it takes to step right back into the classroom and lift the students up on the teacher's shoulders with enthusiasm that sweeps over the students' negativity. For our freshmen to be successful, they need teachers who believe that the subject matter is crucially important. They need teachers who believe that their subject matter will make students' lives better and who will, therefore, do whatever it takes to reach each and every child.

In the movie *Mr. Holland's Opus* (Field, 1996), the principal tells the young Mr. Holland that a teacher has two jobs. One is to "fill young heads with knowledge," but the other is "to give them a compass." In this age of high-stakes testing, the idea of giving students a compass is in many instances taking a back seat, if not being lost altogether. This idea of giving students a compass is exactly what the superintendent of schools in San Diego was talking about when he said, "First we must make students believe they can have access to the American Dream."

I have been guilty of taking a step back from this topic. Years ago, I would refer to this topic as "the soft stuff," as though it was somehow less important than the nuts and bolts of Freshman Transition. However, I now consider it to be the most important part of transitioning freshmen. Imagine what schools in America would be like if all young people had the kind of belief systems that would transform them into *students*. Would your classes be different if students had a respect for concepts like humility, service, and giving?

We would like to suggest that the courage to teach is the courage that it will take to bring a message of belief to a nation of students in need of it. There will be times when we will have to see ourselves as prophets in a world that does not want to hear our message. Still it is a message that needs to be heard. That is why we must be prophets carrying the message of believing to a lost world of at-risk students. It will not be easy and that is why we will need courage to teach it. It is also why a team of teachers working together is such a wonderful tool for conveying this message to our freshmen.

So when we talk about the teacher believing that the subject matter is important, we do mean the subject matter of an English class or an algebra class, but we also mean the subject matter of believing is important.

The second thing that teachers must believe is that the students can learn the subject matter. This idea has been the subject of great debate within the academic community, especially when it comes to certain topics. For example, in recent years most states have begun to require that all students take algebra. I know many teachers who question whether all students can learn algebra. I am an English teacher, and I have no idea whether all students can learn algebra or not. I do know that there are many people who question whether all students can learn grammar as well. However, those questions cloud the real issue in the classroom. That issue is this: If I believe that there are a certain number of students who cannot learn my subject, then I am content when certain individuals do not learn it.

Two years ago, a student who we will call Mary came into my class and presented me with what looked like an academic flat line. She had no interest in English, tried to put her head down all the time, and never knew the answer to any questions I asked. I tried everything with Mary. I e-mailed her mother who shared my concern for her progress. Like every good teacher does, I tried turning this knob and adjusting that lever. It was all to no avail until one day in late January when Mary turned in a paper that was awesome. When I returned the paper to her, I told her that either she had been wasting a great mind or that her mother was a very good writer. Mary's mother e-mailed me to assure me that she did not write the paper.

Mary came alive in the classroom. She began to answer questions, and her answers were deep and insightful. The papers that Mary turned in the rest of the semester were also top notch.

My point is that if Mary's mother and I had just been satisfied with the idea that not all students can learn English, then Mary may never have awakened. As a teacher, I cannot be worried with whether all students can learn my subject matter. Instead I must believe and have enthusiasm that each student in my class can learn what I have to teach. If I do not believe that, I will not be a redeemer of the academic lost, and being a redeemer is the essential job of a great teacher. I believe students can succeed because, to again quote Robert Duvall from *Second Hand Lions*, "Those are the things worth believing in."

Sometimes teachers and parents actually hold students back from success because we are not believers in miracles ourselves. Bob Moore in *You Can Be President (or Anything Else)* (1994) tells how they train fleas for a flea circus. He says even though they can jump the equivalent of a human jumping twenty stories, fleas can be taught not to jump. All one has to do is to put the fleas in a jar and put the lid on. The fleas will try to jump but will smash into the lid time and again. After a while, the fleas learn not to jump so high. Once the learning is complete, the trainer can remove the lid, and the fleas will never jump any higher than the top of the jar.

Ben might have been an example of such training had he not been a believer himself. He had a fine motor skill problem that made it difficult for him to write legibly. He also ran funny and, as a result, was always chosen last for parks and recreation teams. When he was in elementary school, Ben was placed in a handicapped physical education class. However, Ben played football, basketball, and baseball throughout his elementary years. Ben wanted to follow in the footsteps of his older brother who found quite a bit of success in sports. Ben's father did not want him to suffer the disappointment that he knew would come to Ben as he grew older, so he counseled Ben to develop his mind, which his father told him was his natural talent. Ben, however, did not listen, and he continued to play sports every season through middle school. During one basketball game in his eighth-grade year, Ben was able to outplay larger and more skilled players by using his intelligence and the skills he had developed through all those years of playing at the parks and recreation level. After that game, his father began to become a believer. He told Ben that evening that if anyone had ever told him that Ben could play that well, he would have never believed it.

Ben's story is long and followed many crushing setbacks, but Ben used those events to grow stronger. He continued to play multiple sports in high school. When he was a junior, he was given the assignment of defending a Division I bound player who was averaging more than thirty points per game. Ben held him to three points in what Ben's coach called the best game he had ever seen played in his thirty-plus years of coaching. Ben went on lead his baseball team in hitting with a .400 average. His senior year he became the captain of the football team and was also selected second team all-state.

As you may have guessed, Ben is my second son. For much of Ben's life, I was what Bob Moore called "a lid put-er-on-erer." He says we must become "lid taker-off-erers!"

Each one of my children has taught me in their own way that miracles do happen. Many of my freshmen, like Mary, have taught me the same thing. I know now that I must not let my expectations put limitations on anyone. I must believe that every student can learn my subject matter, and I must believe that every student has a miracle inside of him or her because I have seen those miracles happen in my life.

The third major idea that a teacher must believe is that the teacher can make a difference in the lives of the students. I was once asked to speak about motivation and classroom management to high school faculty. When I got to the school on Saturday morning, I learned that I was to address the teachers who the school division considered to be weak, and I was to be their punishment. I expected the day to be a real trial, but I was pleasantly surprised by a group of educators who were eager to find better ways to operate in their classrooms. However, after a day of motivation, one gentleman got up and said, "That is all well and good, but we all know that each of us is only in one-seventh of each school day, and we only teach the child during one school year. There are too many other factors in their lives for us to have any real impact."

I understand that the circumstances he described are real, but I also know that one good teacher in a lifetime can make all the difference in a student's life. Teaching in the same small town the way I have for many years, I have had the joy of working in my yard and having a forty-something man or woman drive up and stop to tell me how much my class meant to them. Sometimes, being a teacher does have its rewards, but more importantly teachers do make a difference, and we occasionally get the opportunity to actually see the difference we make.

THREE THINGS STUDENTS MUST BELIEVE

Just as teachers need to believe in certain ideals, students also have three things in which they need to believe if they are to be successful in a school. Not all students inherently believe what I am about to share. Therefore, it is imperative for a Freshman Transition Program to actively seek ways to get students to believe these ideals.

First, they must believe that they can learn the subject matter. Much is written about learned helplessness. Some of us think that if we do not really try, then we do not really fail. Others suffer from authority figures who only criticize. We often give up because we have not had much encouragement. Most teachers have been in parent-teacher conferences and heard a parent say, "I understand why Johnny cannot learn algebra. I couldn't understand it either." Of course, statements like that not only give Johnny an excuse to not learn algebra, they also create an expectation in his own mind that he will not be able to learn it.

Bob Moore says that the biggest failure of American schools is that they do not teach students the role of failure in success. Fear dominates schools. Students fear teachers; teachers fear students. Students fear other students. But the biggest fear is the fear of failure. Students are afraid to answer questions because they might be wrong. Students are afraid to answer questions because they might be right, and that would not be viewed as cool. Students are afraid to go out for the team because they may be cut. They are afraid to go out for the school play because others might laugh.

There are so many reasons why students do not believe they can learn. The biggest is that if they can learn, then they will have to work. I know this may come as a surprise, but some of our students are afraid of work. When I mention grammar in my classroom, I see a veil go over many students' eyes. They may be able to respond to their name, but their brains disengage. If you ask them, they will tell you that they have never been able to learn grammar, their parents were never able to learn grammar, and their children will never be able to learn grammar. If I do not take time to challenge this notion in my students, and if I fail to convince them that there are things in grammar that they can learn, then they will continue to shut grammar out of their lives. If I fail to point out to them the things that they are learning that they never thought they could, then an opportunity to build enthusiasm for the subject will be lost.

The legendary John Wooden, who led UCLA to nine national basketball championships in ten years, told his players, "Don't let what you can't do get in the way of what you can do." We need to point out to our students what they can do. We need to use this concept because many of our weaker freshmen see any failure as a proof that they cannot learn or that they should give up before their failure is exposed to themselves and to others.

One year in summer school, while we were embracing the wonders of clauses and phrases, one of my students blurted out, "I don't understand!" Another student across the room chimed in, "Yeah, I don't understand, either!" What they really meant was, "You are a lousy teacher!" I could have become angry. I do that on occasion. Or I could have shrunk away and given up. Instead, I challenged the initial blurter. I asked, "What is a clause?" He said, "It is a group of words with a subject and a verb." I responded, "You are a genius! In addition, you do understand what a clause is." I then asked blurter number two, "What is a phrase?" He said, "It doesn't have a subject and a verb." I said, "You are a genius, as well. Now let me tell you what you don't understand. You don't understand predicate adjectives and predicate nominatives, which we studied yesterday. Today, we are talking about clauses and phrases, and you just demonstrated that you do understand clauses and phrases. I am sorry that I was not clear enough about predicate adjectives and predicate nominatives, but the truth is that your life will probably be okay without those. However, punctuation is dependent on an understanding of clauses and phrases, so the good news is you will live a rich and full life knowing the wonders of clauses and phrases. You also have a good foundation for understanding punctuation. By the way, you do understand!"

If our students do not believe they can learn, we must convince them otherwise. It is a daunting yet imperative task if we hope to transition them into successful high school students.

The second thing students must believe is that the system is there for them. Do any of your students spend any time fighting the system? I bet they do. Mine do. As a matter of fact, a former student who we will call Mark spent all of his first freshman year and part of his second freshman year hating the system. He started his second year (his first with me) claiming that everyone in the school was against him because of his ethnicity. It took me more than half of the year to get him to believe that most people did not even know where he was from, and, if they did, they did not even know anything about his country. I could talk and talk with Mark and show him how everyone in the school was pulling for him, and he would come up with yet another example of how he felt someone was out to get him. The truth is that Mark did not want to change. If Mark listened to what I had to say, his whole world would be different, and sometimes that is hard to face. Luckily, though, Mark did begin to listen, and moved on to the tenth grade. As a matter of fact, I believe Mark will go to college. He is brilliant, but his desire to fight the system caused him to miss school, skip classes, misbehave, and regularly get into trouble.

We must spend class time and energy doing things that will make students believe the school is there for them. One of my writing assignments is to tell students that more than $11,000 is spent on each one of them each year to provide a quality education. I ask them to discuss what they think about that. I want them to know that fact. I ask them to discuss what taxpayers should be able to expect for their money. I want students to feel the responsibility that should go along with that sort of financial investment.

Whenever students say something to the effect of "This school sucks," we must take the time to challenge that, too. I like to remind them of the things that the school does for them. As teachers we have to constantly remind students about these things because the normal ninth grader tends to take things for granted. Use time in class to tell your students about the sacrifices another teacher is making. If there is a teacher who works behind the scenes making scholarships available to students, let students know. You do not even have to name the teacher if that teacher would prefer. Just tell the students about something that is going on behind the scenes that you think they should know.

Celebrate all the successes of the school and your students. Sometimes these successes are obvious. For example, occasionally a team will win a state championship, but we also have students working in all sorts of activities that did not win a state championship but who are helping to make our school better just the same. Find ways to make sure students know about this. Make writing assignments about the good things that are going on in the school. Ask school administrators to be a part of your recognition programs. Give them a chance to come into the class occasionally and ask students questions or check their student planners. Have the administrator give prizes to the students who are well-prepared. Do things that tell students that school is a cool place to be and that the system is there for them.

The third, and perhaps most important, thing for our freshmen to believe is that life is or can be good. I believe that many students are chronically depressed. They believe that life is good for others, but their experience in life is that things just do not turn out well for them. They may see life as luck. This perception becomes the root of their academic and social choices. If we are to help such students find success, we must tackle this root problem. We have to show students that life is much less about luck and much more about choices.

If a student believes that life is not good, and there is nothing that the student can do to improve his or her condition in life, then there is no reason to try. Teachers must choose to fashion "teachable moments" in their classrooms to help foster belief systems that help students make the kind of choices that improve their condition in life. When immediate change is unlikely, students need examples of people who had to persevere until their lives improved. The stories that we read in English class must be chosen to illustrate how people can make choices that will change the outcome of their lives. The stories behind historical leaders must be brought out when they can help influence students' belief systems. All teachers can take the time to find opportunities to lift students' belief that life can be good.

If a ninth grader does not enter our high school already in possession of a positive belief systems, where else will they learn one if not from us? If your school has a goal of doing a better job of transitioning its freshmen, then you must first look at what most stands in the way of that transition. It is all about attitude and belief. You can build any master schedule you want, you can place students in any physical location you can think of, but if you do not tackle the main impediments to student success, you have at best given an aspirin to cure a major disease. Our goal as educators, our potential as educators, is to help students find a life-long and lasting cure.

Chapter 13

Closing Thoughts

We hope that from this book you have gained great insight into what you and your school can do to better meet the transition needs of your school's freshmen. We hope that you have found strategies that you can take and make your own for the betterment of your students and your school. To close this book, we have decided to let Ray Moore share his personal perspective on how teaming has not only benefited his school and his students, but also has increased his effectiveness as an educator.

THE POWER OF TEAMING

As you would expect from a career that has spanned more than three decades, my career has enjoyed many ups and downs. When I was asked in 1991 by my school's administration to begin looking into our school's freshman problem, I never would have predicted that I was about to embark on the greatest "up" of my career. That request is what led to my involvement with teaming and transitioning freshmen, and teaming and transitioning freshmen have made the last decade and a half of my teaching career more exciting and rewarding than all the years before.

It seems like many teachers tire out as they reach the end of their careers. Because of teaming, I instead have been energized. The relationships that I have been able to form with team teachers and the strength and ideas I have gained from those relationships have enabled me to be more effective with each passing year.

In *Mr. Holland's Opus*, Richard Dreyfus's character, Glenn Holland, is a high school band instructor. After a long career, Mr. Holland is forced to retire because of budget cuts. In a scene that brings tears to the eyes of even the most stoic, Mr. Holland's former students give him a send off that only Hollywood could imagine.

I have seen many teachers retire over the years, but I have never seen anyone receive a send off like Mr. Holland's. More than likely, I will retire soon, and I do not expect that I will have such an experience either. However, my goal is to be worthy of such an honor.

When I do finally retire, it will not be up to me to judge whether or not I was worthy. What I do know, though, is that if anyone considers me to be so worthy, I will owe much of that to what I have gained from being a part of team.

Bottom line, teaming has made me a better teacher. Ultimately, though, it is not about me. What is most important is that because of teaming, my ninth-grade students have been better served. I have been able to meet better the needs of thousands of young people. While I have in no way done so perfectly, I have done so as well as I have because I have been blessed to be a part of a team.

My hope is that you, too, will have a wonderful experience with teaming and that your freshmen will be better off as a result. And my hope is that as your team turns the ninth-grade problem into the ninth-grade opportunity, your school will be transformed from the bottom up!

About the Authors

Scott Habeeb lives in Salem, Virginia, where he currently is the assistant principal for curriculum and instruction at Salem High School. After graduating from Virginia Tech in 1997, with a bachelor's degree in history and a master's degree in curriculum and instruction, Scott was hired by the City of Salem Schools to teach history as a part of its ninth-grade transition program at Salem High School. Scott taught freshmen for seven years and was a ninth-grade team leader, school Web page designer, and coach before moving into his current assignment in 2004. Scott is responsible for the creation of his school's master schedule, oversees his school's efforts to transition freshmen, and handles ninth-grade discipline.

Ray Moore lives in Salem, Virginia, where he currently is a ninth-grade English teacher and the chair of Salem High School's ninth-grade transition program. Ray was hired by the Roanoke County School System to teach at Andrew Lewis High School in 1971, shortly after he graduated from Virginia Tech with a bachelor's degree in English. In 1977, he began teaching at the newly opened Salem High School. In 1991, Ray chaired a committee to look into Salem High School's "ninth-grade problems." That committee's efforts resulted in the creation of Salem High's ninth-grade transition program. This program quickly became a model for other schools also looking to improve their ninth-grade situation.

Alan Seibert lives in Salem, Virginia, where he currently serves as superintendent of schools for the City of Salem. Prior to being named superintendent in 2006, Alan had been the principal of South Salem School from 2004–2006, an assistant principal at Salem High School from

2000–2004, and before that an assistant principal at Andrew Lewis Middle School from 1996–2000. Alan graduated from Virginia Tech in 1991, with a bachelor's in secondary science education. He was then hired by the City of Salem Schools where he taught ninth-grade earth science at Salem High School. During that time, he worked with Ray Moore and other Salem High School faculty members to develop a ninth-grade transition program. Alan went on to earn a master's degree in educational leadership from Radford University in 1996 and a doctor of education in educational leadership and policy studies from Virginia Tech in 2000.

References

1. Blanchard, K., Lacinak, T., Tompkins, C., Ballard, J. (2002). *Whale Done!: The Power of Positive Relationships*. New York: Simon and Schuster.

2. *Chute, Eleanor. (1999, August 24). Back to school: Ninth grade proves to be a pivotal year for youths. Pittsburgh Post Gazette [Online]. Available: http://www.post-gazette.com/regionstate/19990824ninth3.asp*

3. *Fay, J. & Funk, D. (1998). Teaching with Love and Logic: Taking Control of the Classroom. Golden, CO: Love and Logic Press.*

4. *Field, T., Nolin, M., & Cort, R. (Producers), & Herek, S., & Duncan, P. (Directors). (1996). Mr. Holland's Opus [Film]. Buena Vista Pictures.*

5. *Hertzog, C. J., & Morgan, P. L. (1998). Breaking the barriers between middle school and high school success: Developing a transition team for student success. NASSP Bulletin, 82 (597), 94–98.*

6. *Hertzog, C. J. & Morgan, L. P. (2001). Building Bridges Between Middle Schools and High Schools. Welcome to the Middleweb [Online]. Available: http://www.middleweb.com/INCASEbridge.html*

7. *Hertzog, C. J. & Morgan, L. P. (1997, February). Breaking the Barriers: Transition Practices and Their Effect on Student Success in Grade Nine. A Presentation to the Annual Convention of the National Association of Secondary School Principals, Orlando, Florida.*

8. *Jonsson, P. (2004, March 16). Ninth grade: a school year to be reckoned with. The Christian Science Monitor [Online]. Available: http://www.csmonitor.com/2004/0316/p01s02-ussc.html*

9. Kirschner, D. (Producer), & McCanlies, T. (Director). (2003). *Second Hand Lions* [Film]. New Line Cinema.

10. Kinsella, W.P. (1999). *Shoeless Joe*. Wilmington, MA: Mariner Books.

11. Lan W., & Lanthier, R. (2003). Changes in students' academic performance and perceptions of school and self before dropping out of schools. *Journal of Education for Students Placed at Risk, 8 (3)*, 309-332.

12. McIver, D.J. (1990). Meeting the needs of young adolescents: Advisory groups, interdisciplinary teams and school transition programs. *Phi Delta Kappan, 71 (6)*, 458-464.

13. Moore, B. (1994). *You Can Be President (Or Anything Else)*. Gretna, LA: Pelican Publishing Company.

14. Muir, Mike. (2003, November 24). Research Brief: Teaming and Achievement. *The Principal's Partnership* [Online]. Available: http://www.principalspartnership.com.

15. Orfield, G. (2004). *Dropouts in America: Confronting the graduation rate crisis*. Cambridge, MA: Harvard Education Press.

16. Parker, Palmer. (1997). *The Courage to Teach*. San Francisco: Jossey-Bass.

17. Wooden, J. (1988). *They Call Me Coach*. New York: McGraw-Hill Companies.